BARBARA CARTLAND'S
ETIQUETTE HANDBOOK

BARBARA CARTLAND'S

ETIQUETTE HANDBOOK

A Guide to Good Behaviour from
the Boudoir to the Boardroom

Illustrated by
Francis Marshall

BOOKS

Published by Random House Books 2008

2 4 6 8 10 9 7 5 3

Copyright © Barbara Cartland 1962

Barbara Cartland has asserted her right under the Copyright, Designs
and Patents Act, 1988, to be identified as the author of this work

First published in Great Britain in 1962
by Paul Hamlyn Ltd

This edition first published in 2008
by Random House Books
Random House, 20 Vauxhall Bridge Road,
London SW1V 2SA

www.rbooks.co.uk

Addresses for companies within The Random House Group
Limited can be found at: www.randomhouse.co.uk/offices.htm

The Random House Group Limited Reg. No. 954009

A CIP catalogue record for this book
is available from the British Library

ISBN 9781847945341

The Random House Group Limited supports The Forest
Stewardship Council (FSC), the leading international forest
certification organisation. All our titles that are printed on
Greenpeace approved FSC certified paper carry the FSC logo.
Our paper procurement policy can be found at
www.rbooks.co.uk/environment

Mixed Sources
Product group from well-managed
forests and other controlled sources
www.fsc.org Cert no. TT-COC-2139
© 1996 Forest Stewardship Council
FSC

Printed and bound in Germany by
GGP Media GmbH, Poessneck

CONTENTS

One

GOOD MANNERS

The invisible and indefinable

There is a lot of nonsense talked about etiquette. At bed-rock the word really means good manners; and good manners are merely the evidence of man's civilisation.

The difference between a barbarian and a modern is that the latter is expected to behave in what we call a civilised manner. In other words, he has good manners.

But good manners are not just rules and taboos. Nor are they merely the art of answering an invitation correctly, of knowing how to introduce your friends to one another, in choosing the right expressions in thanking for a party. There is something invisible and indefinable, but very real, about genuine good manners.

When Elizabeth, the Queen Mother, was Duchess of York, a small boy who was presented to her exclaimed afterwards: 'Oh, *what* a polite lady!'

Some years later during the war, when the Duchess of York had become Queen, I was

7

talking about the incident to her sister-in-law and one of her closest friends, Mrs Michael Bowes Lyon.

'When she was only a child, the Queen was noted in Scotland for her exquisite manners,' Mrs. Bowes Lyon told me. 'Everyone who went to Glamis remarked on them.'

Suddenly Colonel Michael Bowes Lyon joined in the conversation and said: 'Elizabeth has always been the same; whenever she meets anyone she invariably wants to give them something.'

I know no better description of good manners than that. They are and should be the outward and visible sign of an inward warmth and generosity.

William of Wykeham's motto for Winchester College 'Manners Makyth Man' meant in the medieval English of his day, 'Character makes a man'. Certainly good manners as we know the word today are a reflection of character.

Too many people believe that 'Manners make a gentleman'. This is a misconception. Manners, in the modern meaning of the word, make nothing. They are a product.

People have tried for centuries to define the word 'gentleman' with varying degrees of wit — from the proverb which says: 'It is not the coat which makes a gentleman', to Michael Arlen, who wrote: 'A gentleman is a man who is never rude unintentionally.'

There is also the twentieth century *bon mot* — 'A gentleman is one who uses the butter knife when he eats alone and has to wash up.'

Perhaps Robert Surtees came closest to a satisfactory definition when he wrote: 'The only infallible rule we know is, that the man who is always talking about being a gentleman, never is one.'

Yet a man can be of gentle birth and a boor by nature. He can be a miner or a dustman and yet be a great gentleman.

To be a gentleman in its finest and best sense is secretly the ambition of every Briton and the standard he desires to attain. Yet perversely we enjoy and admire bad manners. Perhaps it is on a par with the Frenchman who often makes fun of nuns and priests because he is innately religious.

Gilbert Harding was one of the best-known personalities which television ever produced. He was a man of infinite kindness and fundamentally a gentle character. Yet he gained his reputation by occasional outbursts of rudeness.

Sunday night after Sunday night people sat holding their breath in front of their television sets in the hope that 'Gilbert would be in form' — in other words that he would annihilate with a fierce onslaught of words and invective a little man who was evading a question about his particular 'line'.

9

As a nation we enjoy cartoons which cruelly victimise wives dominating their henpecked husbands, interfering dragons of mothers-in-law and pompous politicians.

In the average comedy sketch we watch delightedly the biting wit with which a superior character degrades an inferior. We laugh at the embarrassment of the weak in the presence of the powerful. We have a sneaking regard for the confidence trickster, the defrauder, even the seducer.

Why should we find anything amusing in these unpleasantnesses? Perhaps it is that we admire cleverness in any form whatever, as long as we ourselves are not the victims.

Do we really believe, in our imaginative flights, that life is a battle with no holds barred, where might is right and we can only succeed by trampling on the other fellow?

If we do, it is a subconscious memory of our savage ancestors. Might, as Napoleon, Hitler and a long procession of tyrants typify, is not Right.

The codes of religious belief, of honour, of protecting the weak against the strong, of co-operation, chivalry, tolerance and pity are the things which make life worth living.

I would also add those traits so charmingly described by Malcolm in *Macbeth* as 'the King's becoming graces' — justice, verity, temperance, stableness, bounty, perseverence, mercy, lowliness, devotion, patience, courage, fortitude.

These are all summed up by the phrase Good Manners.

The origin of good manners

You cannot hope to live as a human being without good manners.

Someone once said to me: 'I've no time for the hypocrisy of being pleasant to people I don't feel like being pleasant to!' But he was an embittered and lonely cynic.

Nature intended us to have good manners. If you insist on a scientific practical reason for decent behaviour then ponder for a moment on the instinct of all human beings to collect together in a society.

Long before man could use speech to give it a name, he formed the family, then groups of families became a tribe, and later tribes turned into nations.

The family was the greatest social invention in the history of the universe. If there are intelligent beings on other planets, they may, for all I know, have two heads and six legs, but what is certain is that they must also have invented the family — or the sort of life we call civilised would be impossible.

If you analyse the life of the family, you will find it is based on a mass of unwritten laws or conventions, which is a pompous name for good manners.

You cannot force the family to flourish by legislation. Indeed, we go to law to break it up — by divorce, the State care of the children, putting the old people in a 'Home.' (Note the pathetic attempt to pretend that an Institution can, by being described as a 'Home', be the same as the real living-place of the family.)

The family, and therefore ultimately human happiness, flourishes or withers by the practice of good manners.

That is why I hope you will regard this book as worth reading. If good manners were just a matter of what in the narrow sense of the word is signified by 'etiquette', I would not have troubled to write it.

It is not really important to know the correct way of addressing an Archbishop, whether a cake should be eaten with the fingers or a fork, or if you should put the milk in the tea-cup before or after you have poured the tea. But it is important to cultivate an ability to merge with the pattern of one's fellow human beings without jarring their sensibilities.

I remember when King Edward VIII abdicated and became the Duke of Windsor and married Mrs. Simpson, it was a fiercely debated topic of conversation in London society as to whether one should or should not curtsy to her.

As I had known the new Duchess of Windsor

THE FAMILY

for many years I asked Lady Louis Mount-batten what was correct. She replied:

'As Dickie and I are very fond of the Duke and it will give him great pleasure if his wife receives the same courtesy as we give him, I shall most certainly curtsy to the Duchess.'

That is what makes a book of etiquette so difficult to write. In all our lives there are innumerable occasions when to act correctly is to act wrongly, because it isn't so good-mannered, so tactful or so kind as doing what is, in fact, incorrect.

So don't think that this book can give you rigid rules for good manners. It cannot. It can merely signpost the way, and your heart must do the rest.

You can have laws to control activities, and heaven knows, we have enough of them today. Every one of them says, 'No — you shall not do this.' Very few say, 'Yes — you shall do this.' For what you want to do you have three guides; custom, convention, tradition.

Custom is a living, developing thing. There is nothing very logical about it, but it gives stability.

Convention is a defence against offensive behaviour by oneself or by others. It produces respect from people by making you respect them. Life would be indecent without convention.

Tradition emerges slowly from experience of failure and success. It gives you an anchor in life and provides a set of rules which has in the past proved to be worth following.

Today, unfortunately, we are too bemused with progress. We tend to believe that anything new must, *ipso facto*, be better than the old so that we not only remain ignorant of the heritage of the past with its customs, conventions and traditions, but we do not even trouble to know what they are.

The result is that large numbers of young people take their first steps into social life, whether it is in their first job, at their first dinner, or during their first love affair, in sublime ignorance. They are therefore haunted by the fear that they will do or say something ridiculous or offensive.

If I had to write down the unwritten law of good behaviour in one simple phrase there would be no negative 'You Shall Not', but a strong 'You Shall'. And first and foremost— 'You Shall Possess Tact'.

Unfortunately, tact is not a virtue provided at birth as if it were a talent for painting, acting or writing. Tact has to be learned, from the pages of history, through accepting the unwritten laws of society, by your own trial and error.

We all know the joke about the plumber who burst into an unlocked bathroom, found a woman in the bath and said: 'Beg yer pardon, Sir.'

It is an obvious example of tact which relied on the instinct to spare someone embarrassment.

My grandmother always told the story of how, when she first married, people went out to dinner in their carriages, with a coachman driving and a footman on the box. When they arrived the footman helped wait at the party.

On one occasion at a very grand house, one of the visiting footmen dropped a tray on which he was carrying a priceless Crown Derby dessert service. The hostess, in my grandmother's words, 'never blinked an eyelid' and went on talking as though nothing had happened.

After dinner the visitor who had brought the footman with her tried to apologise and said miserably:

'I am so terribly upset about your lovely dinner service.'

'Please don't worry,' was the answer. 'It was very old.'

This was tact based on an unselfish desire to spare another person. Tact is, in fact, always the subordination of oneself to the needs of others. A selfish, unfeeling person is invariably a tactless one.

All famous hostesses, all good statesmen, all

... DROPPED ... A PRICELESS CROWN DERBY
DESSERT SERVICE

17

successful rulers, all charming and much-liked people are tactful. Tact, indeed, is the real polish on a personality and comes from their best and finest instincts.

Are good manners natural?

Many people think that a display of good manners must be assumed. That does not mean that they reject them, but they imagine that they will be able to utilise this surface-culture rather like putting on a wig. The result is usually slightly comical and the deception obvious.

I like the story of the first Lord Birkenhead who, when visiting America in 1923, played tennis at a country house with two young Americans. He lost the first set and started disastrously on the second. His agitated hostess then approached his daughter and asked: 'Say, is it etiquette for the Earl to be beaten? Because I can easily signal them to lose!'

Society throughout history has, from time to time, attempted to adopt an almost ridiculously rigid code of behaviour. When this happens the social structure eventually collapses. This occurred at the Court of Versailles under Louis XIV and XV when etiquette became complicated beyond all reason. It was somewhat the same during the Regency period in England and is, in a vastly different form, taking place among some members of the younger generation in modern Britain.

Just as the formalism of Versailles and the effete speech of the Regency era gave way to more sincere and less affected customs, so the ritualistic slang, exaggerated dress and bizarre musical taste of some teen-agers succumb to a more flexible code of behaviour later in life.

It will then be as unnatural for their children

EXAGGERATED DRESS AND BIZARRE MUSICAL TASTE

to say 'dig this' or to rock 'n roll as for the present generation to address one another as 'old top' and dance the Black Bottom.

Times change, fashion changes, but one thing remains—the fundamental decency and common sense of the human beings who, sooner or later, elect to throw overboard the pretentious, the hypocritical and the absurd. It is inherent in mankind to be always seeking the simple and the natural.

But don't think for a moment that being natural is being a savage. It's such a long time since we crept around on all fours, lived in caves and ate roots, that any idea that this is the natural way of life for human beings is ridiculous. It is natural, after a development period of a few million years, to be civilised. But being civilised means fitting into your own particular niche in our complicated society.

If you have 'the common touch' you will indeed be able to mix with kings and beggars and show good manners to both. Our own Royalty, for instance, have the gift of mixing with anyone and everyone.

'She's really no different from us,' is a comment repeated in surprise over and over again after the Queen has visited some part of the Commonwealth.

It is the naturalness of the Queen, Prince Philip and the Queen Mother which delights everyone who meets them. It results from unselfconsciousness and an unfailing wish to please.

Sargent, when painting a portrait of the Queen Mother when she was young, said: 'She is the only completely unselfconscious sitter I have ever had.'

She has no BBC accent, no plum-in-the-mouth of pontifical purity, no exaggerated preciousness alleged by the ignorant to go with high birth. The result is a warmth and friend-liness that puts everyone at ease and makes her the greatest ambassador for the British way of life we have ever had.

What a contrast to those people who, frantically trying to be snobs in the misconception that they will be taken as persons of importance, try to get rid of their local accent, exaggerate their aitches and pronounce every vowel through pursed lips! They embarrass their listeners—and to cause embarrassment is an indefensible example of bad manners.

I would much rather hear a person who is too old to change his speech talk ungram-matically than make a bad job of talking properly. It is what you say, not the way you say it, that really matters.

Sincerity is really the only thing that counts in moving people by speaking to them. Abraham Lincoln said at Gettysburg: 'The world will little heed nor long remember what we say here.' But Gettysburg is remembered because what he said there was said with passionate sincerity.

When men speak of what they honestly believe, the inner truth comes from their lips. Then those who listen to them are spell bound. Remember Winston Churchill in the war years lifting the hearts of all who heard him, inspiring, sustaining and invigorating not only the British Commonwealth but the whole of the free world.

Look at Robert Burns and see an amazing phenomenon. He was a ploughman and a dynamic force. He had an exquisite sensibility, he could also be rough, coarse and drunk. But he spoke to 'his own people' in their own language. He never tried to be erudite or pretentious. He expressed his thoughts and feelings in terms familiar to his audience.

'Whatever may be my failings,' he declared, 'may they ever be those of a generous heart and an independent mind.'

He gave expression to emotions which are fundamental and unchanging and that is why, today, he lives, as no other poet lives, in the hearts of Scotsmen all over the world.

I believe that this book will be useful to provide written details of the unwritten code of behaviour. But even though there are sections, sub-sections and an index, the reader will never be able to attain a place of love and respect among his fellow men simply by looking up the code for a given situation.

I think Fray Luis de Leon puts all I am trying to say in one sentence: 'The beauty of life is nothing but this, that each should act in conformity with his nature and his business.'

What is your social class?

Britain is not a classless society, nor is it a triple-class society of upper, middle and working classes. It is made up of scores of classes, each with its own code.

As Cicero said: 'Different manners are given to different pursuits', and you would be foolish to adopt the manners and customs of a class different from your own simply in an endeavour to prove your superiority or inferiority.

You may be surprised to find that anyone could wish to appear inferior. But I suspect that today more bad manners are shown by people pretending to be less important and less aristocratic than they really are, than the reverse.

Members of Parliament lean over backwards to prove that they are representatives of 'the Common Man'. Inherited wealth, a taste for good wine, a wife with a title are concealed by ostentatious economising, insistence on patronising the four-ale bar, and making funny remarks about ancestors who 'were frightful

WHAT IS YOUR SOCIAL CLASS?

rogues, you know!'

It was Lady Astor — the first woman M.P. — who refused to dress down to her constituents and remarked tartly: 'They know I have good clothes, so why shouldn't they see them?'

An East Ham Teddy Boy once said of the Marquis of Milford Haven: 'He's no square, and I likes a chap who is a gent to look like a gent.' At the time the Marquis was visiting a youth club, of which he was president, dressed in immaculate evening clothes, smoking a cigar.

Both Lady Astor and Lord Milford Haven were showing good manners. Why should they insult the intelligence of the people on whom they were calling by assuming what to all intents and purposes would be for them a type of fancy dress?

There are codes which cannot be taught from books but which environment dictates. It would be bad taste, quite apart from being impossible, for a woman to try to dine at Maxim's famous restaurant in Paris on a Friday night in a tweed suit and a hat.

It would be bad taste, though not equally impossible, to sit down to a fish and chip supper in a Blackpool boarding house in full evening dress and a tiara.

Each place has its code of behaviour and to criticise, censure or condemn would be to interfere with every man's right to choose his own amusements and his own companions.

What is the purpose of democracy but to give men and women complete freedom for self-expression and self-development? In totalitarian states men lose not only their freedom but also all the beauty and grace of personal existence.

Good manners exist only where there is freedom. As Rom Landau, the famous Polish author, says in one of his books: 'Wars and their aftermaths always lower the standards and coarsen the grain of human behaviour. They are inimical to all those refinements that we call good manners.'

In the following pages I have set down the accepted standards of behaviour during social contact. They are of necessity generalisations which apply to most people but not necessarily to all.

If your own practice or custom in some specific situation is, and always has been, different, don't change until you have asked yourself this question:

'Has the way I do this appeared to offend friends or strangers, or have I been offended by the same thing from them?'

If you can instantly answer 'no', then ignore the general code and don't worry. If you hesit te, or frankly admit the answer is 'yes', then you can enhance your popularity and, more important, your self-respect—by obeying the code.

The choice is yours. 'This above all, to thine own self be true.'

A FISH AND CHIP SUPPER IN EVENING DRESS

Two

HOME LIFE IS WHAT YOU MAKE IT

Family etiquette

Good manners begin at home. It is a sad reflection that we can be provoked into callous and inconsiderate behaviour more easily by those we love than by anyone else.

When living in the close intimacy of home life, with our parents, our marriage partner and our children, we unwisely expect love to take over from good manners. We know we cannot get along without our own people, but we make no special effort on their behalf.

We unload the burden of the day, release the tensions of business and social life, brush the chips off our shoulders by 'taking it out' on those we love. Then the veneer comes off, and the charming businessman is revealed as a boor, the delightful woman as a carping wife, the amusing children as truculent brats.

The self-discipline of good behaviour should never be dropped within the home, least of all by the husband and wife. It is theirs to set the example of harmony, tolerance, consideration and gentleness which will be reflected in other members of the family, and thereby in the social group and in the nation itself.

Love-making

Women must remember that the act of surrender does not necessarily mean they should abandon all modesty. What often happens is that having once capitulated their bodies they are ready to give themselves without invitation or any pretence at being elusive. The man takes fright at the avalanche of emotionalism and they lose him.

The act of love—in which there need be no reserves, no barriers, no restrictions—should be followed by the woman putting on her elusiveness with her clothes. She should always appear to be the nymph fleeing from the satyr even if she doesn't run very fast! Every time a man makes love to a woman he believes himself the conqueror and the victor. He wishes, too, always to be the hunter, not the hunted.

A woman should never reproach a man for having 'taken' what she has been quite ready to give. Most men dislike talking about the act of love and a wise woman will refer to it only in terms of flattery and love.

At the same time a man is very sensitive about his prowess as a lover and all women should remember this.

If a woman wants to make the ordinary man into a wonderful lover she must praise him continually, showing him how to satisfy her, letting him realise how splendidly he fulfils her dreams.

The slightest criticism will make him reserved and nervous and this is death to physical unity.

On the other hand men should take trouble to find out the vast physical difference between a woman's satisfaction and his own. Lovemaking is an art and without it intercourse can be ugly, frustrating and disappointing.

A man who makes love and turns over or goes to sleep without telling a woman how much he loves her and how greatly he has enjoyed himself is both a fool and a brute. But a woman should also thank the man for having made her happy.

Manners in the bedroom

Good manners in marriage means not taking all the bedclothes in a double bed, not reading if the other partner wants to sleep. The man should open the windows before he gets into bed. A wife should see that the clocks are right so there is no rush in the morning. She should also see that her husband has a clean, aired shirt and fresh socks ready to put on the next day.

It is bad manners for a woman to go to bed

... NOT TAKING ALL THE BEDCLOTHES

with her face covered in cream and equally bad manners for a man who grows hair very quickly to kiss her unless he has shaved.

Cleanliness is one of the essentials of marriage but it is excruciatingly bad manners to leave the bathroom and the basin in a dirty wet mess for the next occupier.

Manners at breakfast

Unless she is ill a woman should get up and cook her husband's breakfast before he goes to work in the morning.

It is bad manners to do this in curlers, without lipstick, in a shabby dressing-gown and down-at-heel slippers.

A man should say 'thank you, darling' for his breakfast and not read the newspaper if his wife is sitting opposite him.

Letters

Marriage partners should never open each other's letters. When they are away from each other a man should write to his wife every day even if it is only a few lines. The same applies to his wife.

Journeys

If a wife goes on a visit to her mother or a friend, the husband should telephone the night she arrives and see if she has got there safely.

If possible he should meet her at the station or the airport when she returns.

A wife should always be at home when her husband returns from a journey. If, unfortunately, there are other people there when he arrives, a wife should excuse herself to be alone with him for a few moments, seeing to his comfort, asking about his travelling experiences and making sure that he is not feeling 'out of it' before she returns to her guests.

Married couples should kiss each other good-bye when either are leaving the home, and kiss each other again on their return. A

... NOT READ THE NEWSPAPER

husband arriving at a party when his wife is already there, greets his host and hostess and then kisses his wife before shaking hands with anyone else. The same applies to his wife if she arrives late.

A wife should rise to kiss her husband when he returns in the evening from work.

Couples who give up their good-night kiss are usually saying good-bye to their marriage.

BAD MANNERS IN MARRIAGE

Here are some of the most widespread examples of bad manners in marriage:

What wives resent in husbands

Wives resent husbands who fall asleep every evening when they are alone with their families, but can be lively, interesting conversationalists when guests are present. Wives loathe the lack of consideration typified by leaving clothes on the floor, the bathroom damp and dirty, cigarette ash everywhere.

What husbands resent in wives

A husband is repelled by a wife who nags or treats him alternately as a child, an idiot, a brute and a tyrant. He resents a wife who doesn't bother to look smart and attractive in the house, but slops about in curling pins, down-at-heel slippers and laddered stockings, with a shining nose and no lipstick.

34

... WIFE WHO DOESN'T BOTHER TO LOOK SMART

Attitude of married couples to each other

'What you are,' said Emerson, 'speaks so loudly that I cannot hear what you say.' This is a comment on behaviour which every married couple ought to bear in mind.

A great many husbands think they are perfect lovers because they give their wives a perfunctory kiss before they leave for the office; and as many wives are convinced that they are behaving lovingly because they constantly prefix a sentence with 'darling'. But they are surprised to find that their partners are embittered about the flight of romance from their married life.

There is constant danger in the home because it is rightly regarded as a place of freedom and relaxation. Too often it becomes a place of licence and self-indulgence.

Nobody expects a man to act like Beau Brummel in private, or a wife to imitate a Vogue model; but good manners should not be thrown off like an overcoat once the front door is shut.

Familiarity between husband and wife

Familiarity is said to breed contempt. Certainly intimacy can encourage lack of consideration. 'That was no lady; that was my wife' is a silly joke, but it unfortunately reflects the feelings of many husbands.

'I've put up with my husband's secret infidelities and his extravagances all my married life,' the wife of a bankrupt told me. 'He's got a lot of faults, but he's always so nice to me in front of people. He will kiss me and put his arm round me and tell me openly that I'm the finest wife in the world. It sounds stupid, but knowing his faults, I still go on loving him.'

If ever there is a time in the life of the most uncouth of people when at least a pretence of good manners is shown it is during courtship. Then a man and a girl take great care about their appearance and personal cleanliness before each meeting. Then they think out what they shall say to one another; they try to show the height and depth of their characters when expressing their hopes and their ambitions.

The first rule for personal behaviour between husbands and wives is to treasure the beauty and spiritual yearning of that awakening love, and to turn it into the strong, enduring and equally beautiful love of married life. 'Most love affairs start with a conversation about God and end with bed,' a modern cynic remarked.

I am sure that the spiritual side of love is destroyed in many marriages entirely by rudeness and contempt. Good manners are the sunshine and the flowers which, if there are enough of them, can transform the barest room into a cathedral of beauty.

Courtesy pays every married man. There is not a wife alive who does not secretly hope to be treated as a queen even if she protests that she does not deserve it. There is not a woman who after many years of marriage would not like to say of her husband what Mary Anne Beaconsfield said of the courteous Disraeli.

'Dizzy has always given me love, comradeship, trust and good manners.'

Appearance

Oscar Wilde said: 'It is only shallow people who do not judge by appearances.'

I hate the type of boorish individual who, I am told, has hidden beneath such a rough surface a heart of gold. Quite frankly, I am a busy person and I have no time to dig.

Inevitably there will be times when your wife sees you as you would not like others to see you. But make sure that these times are kept to a minimum. Washing, shaving and hair brushing are tasks to complete as early as possible, not delayed or omitted because only your wife will see you.

Nothing looks so unpleasant as a man with twenty-four hours' growth of beard, and the type of husband who doesn't shave on Sundays is not confined to any particular class. Many men are both lazy and slovenly by nature.

By all means be casual and comfortable at

weekends and holidays. But there is a difference between casualness and being unkempt. When you go fishing, help a neighbour to change a tyre or mow the lawn, you can manage to wear old clothes with an air. Do the same when your wife is the only audience.

Cleanliness

Men fondly believe, because advertisers have found it more profitable to direct their appeals and warnings to the more sensitive sex, that body odour is something quite foreign to the human male. Every woman, if she were not so polite, would tell you otherwise.

Viscount Castlerosse, the witty Irish peer who became a journalist, once said:

'A civilised man bathes every day, a man who should be pitied for his absence of any sense of shame bathes once a week, and I suspect that there are subhumans who never bathe at all.'

How clean are you? Make a list of the times yesterday that you washed your hands. When did you last soap yourself all over? The Greeks and Romans, having no soap, relied on loosening dirt by having a slave scrape them with a device called a strigil. They were a clean race. Can we claim to be the same with every possible modern device to help us?

Mannerisms

We all have them—the finger-clicking, nose-rubbing, sniffing, throat-clearing, head-tilting absurdities which we ourselves hardly notice, but which can drive the observer to distraction.

Friends and colleagues may have to endure them now and then. Your wife has to live with them. Think about yours, identify them, and cut them out. If you decide that you have none, ask your wife— and don't fly off the handle when she mentions a few.

And don't believe her when she kindly adds: 'But they don't matter; they're part of you.' They do matter.

Gestures of affection

You probably remember that there were many words, glances and gestures which delighted your wife when she was just your girl-friend or recently your bride. Maybe some were silly and youthful (your wife will not agree), but they all produced a reaction of affection or desire. Continue to use them, adapt them, change them—but don't drop them.

Ignore any rule of etiquette which may say that kisses, arm holding, and terms of endearment are not for use in public. To a woman, a man who suddenly drops his reserve and says, 'Darling, I do love you', regardless of where they are, is a thrill beyond compare.

Likewise a woman will adore a husband who is not too shy to put his arm round her in front of his friends, and who will kiss her passionately at an airport or on a railway station.

'Richard is a wonderful husband in many ways,' a wife told me; 'but I always resent the fact that he never takes his hat off when he leaves me or when we meet in the street. To other women—yes; but not to me!'

Dirty stories and swearing

Plenty of husbands recount what used to be called 'Smoking Room' stories to their wives. Usually they are disappointed at their lack of response. Women have a different sense of humour from men, and it is rarely a bawdy one.

Culprits may suggest that a wife is a pal and they like being perfectly natural in her presence. But I have never met a raconteur of lewd stories who was pleased when his wife took over the same role.

Too many husbands also use bad language in front of their wives.

'I loathe hard-riding, hard-swearing men,' an Edwardian beauty announced when she ran away with an artist. Today bad language is often a habit and sometimes an affectation.

In the army, swearing is something of a pose. 'I'll-show-the-world-I'm-tough' is the idea behind it. But in civilian life it is unnecessary, and, as an old woman in the East End said about her notoriously foul-mouthed husband:

''im! 'es got no vocabulary; that's what's

wrong with 'im.'

Sex

'You make love to me as if you were taking a drink,' said a middle-aged wife in a recent TV play.

Sex, whatever the male may think, is not just a biological urge—at least not under an arrangement where one man and one woman want to sustain and increase physical affection for life. It is an art.

To women, love and sex are one and the same. John Barrymore summarised a man's attitude in saying:

'The thing that takes up the least amount of time and causes the most amount of trouble is sex.'

Perhaps time is the great fundamental difference between the man who says, 'That's that' and a woman to whom every act of love is a momentous, soul-stirring adventure.

You may not think that the most fundamental functions of the adult male and female can possibly be affected by etiquette. In fact, there is probably no human activity so thoroughly encompassed with conventions and taboos. These are designed partly to safeguard the continuance of the race and also to embellish what is a basically physical action with the magic of spiritual attraction.

This is not a book concerned with the details

of sexual behaviour. I merely suggest that husbands should remember to be lovers, in thought and word as well as in deed.

Nothing can be coarser or cruder than a man who satisfies himself without a thought for his wife. No man can be excused for later omitting the small courtesies of gratitude, tenderness and consideration. On these, more than on anything else, rests a happy marriage.

As Norman Douglas says, 'I should be interested to discover what proportion of unsatisfactory marriages is due to the bare fact that the male partner does not know his business.'

A husband's help in the home

A misguided idea of the twentieth century is that a considerate husband is a home slave. The aproned male over the sink is as contemptible as the contrasting figure of his nineteenth century great-grandfather, who called his wife a chattel and used her as such.

When wives work, it may be reasonable for husbands to shoulder some of the household chores; but a man who loves his wife will perform them as a gesture of assistance and not carry them out as a duty.

A woman wishes to respect her man. She wants to regard him as the builder of her home and leader of the family unit. She also, if she is feminine, likes a 'master'. 'Be kind, be understanding, but be firm' is the motto every man should take when he marries.

'Women are seldom merciful to a man who is timid,' Bulwer Lytton wrote; and in my

THE APRONED MALE OVER THE SINK

experience the happiest marriages are always where the man has the brains, the money and the ambitions.

Emancipation may have brought women votes, higher education and careers, but it has certainly not brought them the happiness of being a fragile, delicate little woman protected and looked after by a big strong man.

Money

It is insulting to regard a wife as a kept woman. She is entitled to have her own income for her own personal needs and to spend it without question and without inquests. The nicest gesture of respect a husband can give to his wife is to regard her as his financial partner in the marriage. A spontaneous, regular allowance of 5s. a week is an indication of a better mannered marriage than £5 which has to be wheedled and explained.

Wives must note, however, that the regular housekeeping money belongs to the husband and anything 'snitched' from this allowance is returnable should he demand it.

ADVICE TO WIVES

Appearance

Women may marry men for their money, character, or social position. Men marry women for their looks. All women know this and make the very best of their appearance in order to attract men.

Too many forget that it's easy to catch a husband and hard to keep one. A man pays all his life for the pretty face which has lured him up the aisle. A clever wife will never for one moment let him suspect he has got a bad bargain.

A Frenchman wrote: 'Love lessens the woman's refinement and strengthens the man's.' Far too many women become unrefined when they have landed their fish.

There is nothing improper in being naked and it can be very attractive. A woman can also be entrancing and desirable half-dressed. But no woman, not even a model in a lingerie establishment, has managed to look attractive when wriggling in or out of a suspender belt.

'What a pretty nightgown!' I said to the wife of a very attractive politician. 'It's my best,' she answered. 'I don't wear it at home— I keep it for staying away.'

Just because you're alone with your husband and not expecting company is no excuse for not looking neat and tidy.

'Women were made to give our eyes delight;
   A female sloven is an odious sight.'

Cleanliness

Modern women are cleaner and healthier than they have ever been. It is hardly necessary to point out that the reason for cleanliness is a consideration for others more than a regard for one's health. But it may be worth bearing in mind that water is still the best source of hygienic cleansing of the skin. Beauty products should be an addition, not a replacement.

In the same way scents, whether on powder or liquid bases, are to enhance a woman's presence, not to disguise a smell.

If your husband doesn't smoke, give it up. I think anyway, that no woman should smoke because the smell of tobacco lingers on her skin and in her hair. Women's clothes also smell of stale smoke, and a mixture of cheap Virginia tobacco and French scent can turn the strongest stomach.

Lelord Kordel in his book *Lady Be Loved* writes:

'No woman who offends the masculine nose or eye can be truly desirable,' and he goes on to speak very forcibly of the women who offend through lack of cleanliness in personal and intimate hygiene.

The common defect among many women who are otherwise particular is to omit regular shampooing. Talk to the average hairdresser's assistant and she will tell you some horrid facts about her clients. The reason is, of course, a too tender regard for a perm or a set.

If you expect your husband to enjoy kissing your face and to go to sleep on the next pillow, you will accept that a pleasantly smelling head is more attractive to him than the most undulating wave. If, therefore, you cannot afford both, it should be obvious which to choose.

Mannerisms

These are common to both sexes, so read, mark and learn the hints for husbands under this heading and don't placate yourself by wondering why men are so funny. Women aren't funny with their mannerisms; they are simply infuriating.

Gestures of affection

Society insists, and rightly, that woman receives and man gives. Be reserved with your caresses and tokens of affection in public, although you should be ready to accept them with delight should your husband offer any.

In the wedding ceremony you agreed to give as well as to receive. It is neither human nor honourable to play 'hard to get' once a proposal has been accepted, confirmed and consummated. Besides, it is dangerous. There are plenty of women only too ready to give without legal or religious provisos.

In the privacy of the home regard a kiss for your husband as more than a conventional ritual or a sort of matey 'hail and farewell'. The kiss is a sex symbol of flesh to flesh and there is nothing improper or untimely in practising it at any time of the day or night.

'Kissing is a means of getting two people so close together that they can't see anything wrong with each other,' an American says, and we all know that a kiss solves an argument better than any judge.

A kiss should also be a two-way activity. A rebuff is bad form, and I consider that the cheek-tilting action practised by so many wives is tantamount to a rebuff.

Talk

Ask any man the most usual marriage fault of women and he will almost inevitably say, 'nagging'. If you can say only things which are critical, then don't say anything. Any fault of taciturnity will be so unusual that it will be readily forgiven. Most women talk too much anyway, and some of the talk is bound, rightly or wrongly, to be described by the average husband as nagging.

Sex

Sex snobbery is probably the most objectionable of all feminine behaviour traits in marriage. It is the perfect example of snobbery, for it inevitably takes one of two forms, or sometimes even manages to combine both.

The theory runs on the lines of 'Sex is a common, dirty urge found among the lower classes, whose only interests are beer and bed,'

49

A KISS IS A TWO-WAY ACTIVITY

or 'Society is rotten through the preoccupation with sex of the rich and leisurely, who have nothing better to do.'

After adopting this attitude the Sex Snob smugly tells herself, and probably implies it to her friends, that 'she is above all that sort of thing.'

There is no breach of manners worse than discussing the intimate sex details of your married life with anyone, even your closest friends. There is nothing so low as the type or woman who either sniggers or boasts about sex.

A wife's work in the home

After a long, long battle woman has attained a position of partnership with man in marriage. Compared with the servitude of the past, it has brought duties and codes of behaviour which are appallingly intricate. Such is the price of privilege.

Consideration for others, in this case for each other, which is the basis of good behaviour, should be the golden rule to show the way through the most complex of problems.

Thus a husband, unless he is a boor or an autocrat wants neither a servant nor a toy. He wants his home run well, but without his wife becoming a slave to her sink and brooms. He wants to enjoy her presence without her behaving like a temperamental mistress.

A wife's work in the family is clearly defined by tradition and necessity. Most husbands work

'DARLING, I'VE HAD SUCH A HORRID DAY...'

pretty hard and it is unjust and degrading that they should feel the need, or be told the benefits, of taking on part of the wife's work as well.

Unfortunately, some women are household cheats, and they will strive by every means they can to avoid what they call the 'monotony' of housework. Once they get a man to the sink, he is lost, for they will batten on his good nature relentlessly.

A husband returning home from the office should beware of the soft, weak voice which says: 'Darling, I've had such a horrid day...'

Money

Love of money can easily oust love of husbands. If the former is the greater, then by all means get a divorce, take a job, grow rich and very lonely. If you love your husband and want to remain in love with him—and he with you—then it is probably expedient and considerate to ignore the attractions of work for married women and resolve to be a whole-time wife instead of a part-time wage slave.

'For better, for worse' means precisely what it says. Love is far less liable to fly out of the home where there is poverty than it is to leave a house where the wife is too busy at work to run her home and welcome back her husband.

Three

AS OTHERS SEE YOU

Many married couples who get on perfectly well together find an imp of mischief on their shoulders when other people are present.

'We against the world' is the desirable motto for families in their relationships with other people. Arguments in which a husband and wife take opposing sides are best avoided, for arguments are liable to get more vehement than expected. Angry gibes between married partners are extremely embarrassing to other people.

Criticism

Criticism of one's partner in public is, of course, taboo. No matter how close the friendship, no husband should essay witty remarks in the presence of a third party about his wife's clothes nor she about her husband's stodgy views. I loathe the husband or wife who correct each other's stories. 'No, dear, it wasn't Wednesday, it was Thursday,' is bad manners; so is 'that fish gets bigger every time John talks about it!'

Description of husbands and wives

Many couples are in a genuine quandary trying to decide what to call their partners when mentioning them to others. 'Hubby', 'the old man', 'my better half', 'the missus' and similar terms must not be used. 'The wife' is also wrong.

In shops and in general business activities, where the name of the speaker may not even

ANGRY GIBES BETWEEN MARRIED PARTNERS

be known, it is correct for a husband or wife to say 'Mrs Jones' or 'Mr Jones', but that form of reference is otherwise used only when addressing one's household staff.

At all other times it is correct to say, 'my wife' or 'my husband'.

In speaking to a servant about a Lord, Viscount, Earl or Marquess, the hostess will say: 'Lord X will be called at 9 o'clock' or, 'Please pack for Lord X' but the servant will refer always to 'his Lordship'.

In the case of a Duke, the hostess says 'His Grace'.

Use of Christian names

The use of Christian names has grown tremendously since the war. Some discrimination is needed about this, but no hard and fast rule can be laid down.

It is correct that the older and more important person should suggest that Christian names be used. But where two men or two women know each other well enough to use Christian names, it is sometimes difficult for their respective partners who are not so well acquainted.

Courtesies to wives

Men who are perfectly well aware of the public courtesies normally accorded to women sometimes tend to forget them in the case of their wives, even in public.

When George VI came to the throne, he changed a convention that was probably as old as the monarchy. Quietly, but firmly, so that everyone marked the fact, he insisted on his wife taking precedence over him on informal occasions. Thus Queen Elizabeth would go before him to her theatre seat; would emerge first from the Royal Box at Epsom; would walk slightly ahead of him up the aisle of a church.

It was the regard of a remarkable gentleman for his wonderful wife. If a King of England can regard his wife as of more importance than himself, so can the average husband, with the certainty that he, too, will be regarded as a gentleman.

There is very little inconvenience in rising momentarily from one's chair when your wife returns from shopping. It is only a matter of taking two paces to get on the outer side of her on the pavement. The car will start five seconds later than otherwise if you open the near-side door, see her seated and close it after her before you get behind the wheel.

She will appreciate your courtesy in rising when she leaves the restaurant table to 'powder her nose' and doing the same when she returns. She will like it even more if you remember to open the door for her, help her on with her coat, take her arm on steps and stairways just as you did before you married her. Note that all these things are the ordinary good manners which you will be expected to offer any woman with whom you are in company.

In-laws and relatives

Every engaged man and girl and every newly-wed goes through misery about the correct

... OPEN THE NEAR-SIDE DOOR ...

method of addressing the partner's parents.

A young man should certainly address his prospective father-in-law every now and again as 'Sir'. But most of the time, if he uses any name at all, 'Mr and Mrs Jones' will obviously meet the case.

It is definitely not correct to call your in-laws 'Mother' or 'Father' when the wedding has taken place. Sometimes other names are suggested like Madre, Mater, Pop or Pater. On the whole it is better and more correct to call one's in-laws 'Mr and Mrs' although an increasing number of sons- and daughters-in-law use their parents-in-law's Christian names. By general usage this is acceptable provided the older people do not mind.

The use of the full term 'mother-in-law' or 'father-in-law' which has been bruited because Dr Dale of *The Dales* does so is to be deprecated. I suspect that this use is for clarity of the plot, not as an example of good manners.

In a similar way the whole retinue of aunts and uncles, cousins, nephews and nieces are adopted by the in-law partner. He or she has become one of the family and therefore uses the name normal among the family members of his or her generation.

Mothers-in-law

Mothers-in-law have become a joke and a term of contempt. But for every mother-in-law who

MOTHERS-IN-LAW HAVE BECOME A JOKE

causes trouble there are ten thousand whose quiet, self-sacrificing affection heals the breaches in marriage. A mother-in-law is expected to be the unpaid baby-sitter, the adviser in making ends meet, the money-lender who charges no interest, and the wise counsellor when things go wrong.

But there are three rules which all mothers-in-law must obey.

1. Never visit the young couple without an invitation.
2. Never interfere in their household arrangements.
3. Never criticise.

It is kind, as well as good manners, for a young wife to ask her husband's mother regularly to the house and at some time during the visit to leave mother and son alone together. Young women should always remember that one day they will be mothers-in-law and they should therefore do as they would be done by.

Fathers-in-law

They are expected to pay up. They should also remember that their little girl is grown up and that the young man who loves her is not a big bad wolf.

Servants

Only a few people today are fortunate enough

to have living-in servants, who are no longer called servants but 'the staff'. Nearly everyone, however, will at some time or other come up against social problems connected with the 'daily', the 'by-the-hour' gardener, or the 'char'.

It should be obvious that to retain the services and remain in the good graces of these invaluable people the old-fashioned autocratic attitude is as dead as Victorian bustles. In any event, and it is an example of the way etiquette changes, it is no longer good manners to 'keep people in their place'.

'I'm the cleaning lady wot does for the woman in the next flat' is an unfortunate but true example of the topsy-turvy situation that has arisen.

It behoves the 'woman', in either flat, to behave and speak in a way that proves she is a lady —and her husband a gentleman.

Today, until there is a friendly relationship born of continued knowledge and mutual respect, every man and woman doing a job for you, however menial, is entitled to be addressed by his or her surname with Mr or Mrs in front. Teen-age girls, should they by chance undertake such work, may prefer their Christian name to 'Miss Smith', but it is unlikely.

Later, much later, even elderly women may like to be called by their Christian names, and the average gardener or the man who comes

to clean the car generally has no objection to
the man-to-man atmosphere suggested by his
employer calling him by his surname, plain and
simple.

Female servants should always receive orders
only from the wife; males from the husband.
If occasion arises for one or the other to pass on
an order then it should be 'Mr Brown wants
you to...' or 'Mrs Brown asked me to tell you
that...'. These days it is rarely possible to say
'your master' or 'your mistress'.

Staff

If, however, you have living-in staff, here is
the order of precedence and the manner in
which they are addressed.

Housekeeper (almost an extinct race) is called
Mrs by her employers and the staff whether she
is married or not.

Cook-Housekeeper is called Mrs by her employers and the staff whether she is married or not.
In speaking to the staff of the Cook-Housekeeper the employers say 'Mrs X'.

Butler (more usually a manservant these days)
is called by his surname only by his employers
and 'Mr' by the staff.

Lady's maid (practically non-existent) is called
by her surname by her employers and Miss by
the staff.

Housemaid if elderly is called by her surname
by her employers and Miss by the staff—if

young, by her Christian name by everybody. *Footman, Boot-boy, Odd Man etc.* are called by their Christian names by everybody. All the rest of the living-in staff are called by their Christian names.

Foreign staff. Most people these days employ one or two foreigners in place of the afore-mentioned staff. These are usually called by whichever name is the more easily pronounced.

Au pair

This system, meant to provide mutual help for both the hostess and her foreign guest, has unfortunately become quite the worst example of British bad manners, causing much inter-national bad feeling.

The simple dictionary definition of the term is 'to have board and lodging but to be unpaid for services rendered.' What most people tend to forget is that the phrase literally means 'on a par' — i.e. to treat as an equal.

So disgraceful have been the manners of some British families that in many countries, on the advice of the local priest, girls are warned against coming to Britain 'au pair'.

Too many people have regarded the desire of a foreign girl to broaden her mind by travel, to learn English, or merely to maintain herself at some period between school and college or while awaiting a job, as a heaven-sent chance to exploit her as a cheap servant.

Generally speaking, the sort of girl who comes to Britain to live 'au pair' is the social equal of any middle class family. Certainly, many prove themselves far better bred in the way that they endure brash treatment and suffer

AU PAIR

overwork without complaint.

It is not merely good manners but fundamental humanity to treat a girl who is usually under twenty-one with the consideration one would show to one's own daughter or niece.

She expects, rightly, to be treated as one of the family, have meals with them, and to be addressed by her Christian name.

She should not be expected to wear a dress which insinuates she is a servant, be banished from the dining-room and sitting-room when guests come, or be sent to her room in the evenings.

At the same time it is obvious, by the very nature of her visit, that she is not really one of the family. She should be given the freedom to go out if she wishes and she should have a comfortable room where she can sit as well as sleep. Because she is a girl, young, and in a strange land, some discreet supervision must be made for her welfare, both moral and physical.

It is probable that her religion will be different from that of her host, and it is a kindly gesture to approach a local priest of that religion and mention that the girl is living in your house; failing that, a formal note to the nearest consular official of her country of origin is advisable.

Periodically, a brief and friendly letter to the girl's parents should be written, reporting in general terms and not giving any impression of spying or interfering.

The fact that some of these girls find the freedom of a foreign country goes to their heads, that some may fail to keep their side of the contract as regards baby-sitting and sharing in household chores, does not affect the basic need for good manners to be shown even in return for bad. Kindness invariably breeds kindness, and before criticising it is as well to bear in mind what the behaviour of one's own teen-age daughter would be in similar circumstances.

If a wife and mother regards the 'au pair' guest as a helpful friend and not as a replacement for a servant then all should be well. She should be expected to share the work, but not to do it all. And finally, let me reiterate that she merits many of the privileges of a guest and has no duty to demean herself as a servant.

Treated decently, the 'au pair' girl will return as an unofficial ambassador of her temporarily adopted country. Treated as she unfortunately often is, she goes back reporting that Britain is a nation of ill-mannered boors bent on exploiting foreign girls on the cheap.

The behaviour of 'au pair' hosts and hostesses is often the result of stupidity rather than greed. Some agencies list the names of girls along with ordinary wage-earning servants, and applicants imagine that 'au pair' is just some fancy name for a foreign servant. Some of the girls whose names prospective hosts obtain by advertisements in the European press have no illusions: they adopt the 'au pair' system because it effectively obviates labour laws and awkward questions from immigration officers. Obviously such girls are not the types one wants. But the others who are caught by the specious advertisements have no conception of what is unfortunately involved in coming to Britain 'au pair' in some households.

There are some non-profit organisations, and many agencies working under rigid rules set down by their professional association, which carefully vet both girls and prospective host.

There are also advertisements—both 'wanted' and 'offered'—in the better class of Sunday newspapers. The latter do enable both parties to obtain some details before any arrangement is made.

In any event, whether the girl is a minor or over twenty-one, some correspondence should be entered into with parents or guardian, and references should be exchanged.

It is usual for the 'au pair' visitor to pay her fare *both* ways, but the return fare can be a problem·if the girl does not keep a financial reserve. It may therefore save considerable trouble by arranging beforehand to pay the return fare, keeping this expense in mind when discussing the topic of pocket money.

And pocket money it should be. The girl

should not be expected to pay for her own laundry, shoe repairs, or personal requisites like soap and so on. The money she is given is for luxuries, outings and gifts.

It is very difficult to suggest a figure. There are cases of girls enduring misery on a few shillings a week and of girls kicking over the traces because they have had £5 a week to throw away. Probably £2 to £3 a week is fair, with perhaps an occasional money gift for a hair-do or special outing.

All these things must be settled in writing with the parents or guardian beforehand, and some clear indication given that she will come with an adequate supply of clothes suitable for the changing seasons, or the money to buy them. An outline of the cost of things in this country would be helpful.

Tradesmen

Relationships with tradesmen should be adapted according to the position of the caller. The shop-owner is today the social equal of his customer. To be 'in trade' has long since ceased to be socially inferior, although the way in which many silly people treat shop-keepers and their assistants shows that the attitude dies hard.

In County towns and districts the local shop-keepers are often of Civic importance, being Councillors, Governors of Schools,

Chairmen and Members of various organisations like the Chamber of Commerce, and Trades Council. When writing to them, they are therefore usually addressed as *Esq*.

Neighbours

One cannot choose one's neighbours. On the assumption that misanthropists would select a home in the Western Highlands or the middle of Dartmoor there is a tacit agreement to like the people next door, whether the division is a party wall or a large garden.

In no case is the proverb about it 'taking two to make a quarrel' more true than in the case of neighbourly disputes. Two well-bred fami-

THE SHOP-OWNER IS TODAY THE SOCIAL EQUAL
OF HIS CUSTOMER

lies cannot quarrel; nor can a single ill-bred one.

Whatever one's private thoughts about a neighbour's activities and behaviour may be, they should be kept to oneself. To grumble to another neighbour is bad manners and also bad policy.

Calling on next door neighbours

In the United States it is good manners to call on new neighbours within twenty-four hours of their arrival or one's own arrival. Subsequently an open-door policy applies to both families—and this is literal, for it would be regarded as stand-offish to wait after knocking, and probably even to knock at all.

In Britain the home is still regarded as a castle, and the privacy should be respected. There is no hurry to get acquainted, but the first move must come from the neighbour who was there first.

If the established neighbour makes no move, there is nothing to do but say 'good morning' when meeting and await developments; but most people will ask new neighbours to visit them informally.

'My husband and I wondered if you would care to come round for a drink tomorrow evening' is the usual invitation for one wife to extend to the other.

Don't try to make a big impression which may intimidate your new neighbours and which you may not be able to keep up. If you don't normally have sherry, gin and so on in your home, then make the drink coffee or tea if that is your evening custom.

Indicate a time well after your evening meal and all you need provide is a few simple sandwiches, cakes or biscuits. Dress as you would for any evening at home. Do not ask other neighbours as well. It is their privilege and duty to make friendly overtures to the new-comers, not yours to force them to do so.

Talk about the district, the houses, the shops and similar details. Do not discuss the other neighbours except in response to direct enquiries (which are in fact not in good taste on the part of your guests) and then only in factual terms, without expressions of opinion about their habits, social status, and so on.

Times to leave

Your guests should not stay above an hour or so.

I would like to stress here how important it is to know when to leave. I am always suffering from people who call to see me for 'a little chat' and stay for hours.

Here is a simple guide for guests:

If you are asked to coffee at 11 a.m., you must leave at 12 noon.

If you are asked to lunch at 1 o'clock, you leave at 2.30 p.m.

If you are asked for a drink at 6 o'clock, you

...GOOD MANNERS TO CALL ON NEW NEIGHBOURS

leave about 7.30 p.m.

If you are asked to dinner at 8 o'clock, you leave at 10.30 p.m.

If you are asked in after dinner, you leave at the same time, unless you are pressed to stay to watch the end of a television play or to finish a rubber of bridge.

These times must be flexible, for bed-time and meal-time routine varies from place to place and from class to class. In some circles

PEOPLE WHO STAY FOR HOURS !

it is no doubt perfectly normal for people to eat at 9 p.m. and to regard the night as young at midnight. In the suburbs and the country, where the next day's work may start earlier, people may dine as early as seven and 11 p.m. is late for going to bed.

No hostess could feel her guests had enjoyed themselves if they left before she expected; her depression when this happens is probably as severe as the boredom she has to endure from guests who just don't know when their company begins to pall!

The responsibility is therefore on the guest. 'I really must go; it's getting terribly late, but time passes so quickly when one is enjoying oneself' is the sort of vague remark he can make. The hostess can show genuine disappointment, half-hearted denial, or restrained agreement in her reaction to this comment—and the guest can then act appropriately.

It is not supposed to be correct for a hostess to hint that it is time for her guests to leave; but I regret to say that in my house if people over-stay, my husband gets restless and starts emptying the ashtrays into the fire!

THE HOME

Decorations in the home

Good taste in decoration and furnishing schemes speak louder than the words of the home owners as regards their breeding.

Unfortunately, neither the furniture and decorating industries nor the magazines displaying their wares can be relied upon to provide a source of good taste. Much of what is contemporary and modern is in execrable taste, largely because it is ostentatiously expensive and blatantly novel.

'When in Rome, do as Rome does' is a fairly safe policy. If you dwell in a service flat in an exclusive district then Italian-style plastic furniture, fibreglass tables and dividing walls of aluminium may be all right—your neighbours will have the same thing.

If you live in suburbia, such a motif would be incongruous, arousing misguided envy or irrepressible amazement in the minds of your neighbours—both being emotions engendered by your lack of sensitivity to environment.

What is unforgivable is to endeavour to use your home for some other purpose than the primary one: a comfortable shelter from the outside world.

But plenty of people do contrive other uses: to indicate their wealth, their origin, their social superiority, or their business and social contacts. All of these are not merely bad manners, but they also damage the primary purpose of comfort by making guests feel uncomfortable.

We all know the type of woman— and take good care not to visit her more often than we can possibly help—who goes out of her way to explain that the carpet, which looks just like the Indian ones piled high in every department store, was actually hand-made in a hill village where her dear father was District Commissioner, and is insured for £2,000! Or the man who has a quite illegal coat of arms—unless he is paying the licence fee—on the chimney piece and in appropriate places on books and trinkets simply because he is remotely connected to an extinct Irish peerage.

Or the couple who prominently display signed photographs of important personages who would be surprised to know that they knew them.

Humour is another way to lapse from good manners in the furnishings and decorations. Everyone knows the sort of thing: they are usually sold in tourist centres and seem excruciatingly funny when one is on holiday.

I can see no social advantage in installing a toilet-roll holder bought in Lucerne which plays music when the roller moves. I cannot see the point of hanging a fake Victorian sampler in the hall which advertises one's economic status with the words 'God bless our mortgaged home'. Nor do I like those chi-chi plaques for affixing to doors which by allegedly humorous illustrations indicate whether the door opens on a lavatory, bathroom or bedroom.

Where decorations are concerned, home life is fraught with danger. The paint manufacturers bring out more and more colours and they have to sell them. If they can persuade you that five different colours in one room are smarter than two, then they will have sold three extra supplies of paint.

If the wallpaper manufacturers convince you that it is the done thing to have two walls in one design and the other two in two more, then they will not worry that you have parts of the rolls of paper to throw away. Nor will either of these industries be dismayed at the fact that you soon find your decorative scheme so impossible to live with that you feel you must have the place done over twelve months later.

Ignore all the bright articles and surveys which announce that this year's colour is blue or that a fashionable interior decorator, of whom you have never heard but who is reputedly known to half a dozen millionaires with Riviera villas, insists that clashing colours are stimulating, and dirty white is restful.

All these novelties may be delightful when viewed for ten minutes in an exhibition. Blue may indeed be this year's colour for bedrooms. But you will have to live with these colours and you will presumably hope that the new scheme will last for three years or so.

If you have the opportunity, before decorating, visit one or two of the Stately Homes. Later, ask yourself what the basic colour scheme was and it is almost certain that you will not be able to say. Walls and ceilings of ivory white, pale cream, greenish-white—these are the colour schemes of the master craftsmen of the past. Their taste was perfect. Their decorative schemes were a self-effacing background for the furniture and furnishings.

If your guests go away and when questioned confess that they cannot recall the colour scheme of the rooms they entered at your house—but they remember the charming curtains or the Welsh dresser—then you have the certainty that your decorative scheme was in good taste.

It will be flattering if they single out one or two things for mention in that way. Most homes are overfurnished, looking messy and cramped.

It is far better to have little furniture and good than to cram the place with shoddy rubbish. What is more, antique furniture in oak, mahogany or walnut will always increase in value.

Names of rooms in the home

For the record, the word 'parlour' is not used, nor is the relatively recent, insidious 'lounge', except about airports, hotels and liners. If you have a drawing-room, i.e. a withdrawing room originally intended for the ladies to go to while the men drank their port and smoked their cigars—then call it that. If you have a sitting-room where you sit, watch television and entertain, then call it the sitting-room.

The room where you eat and which has a table is the dining-room—nothing else.

The 'smallest room' in the house is not 'the toilet', 'the W. C.', 'the end of the passage', 'the powder room'. It is the lavatory. And there is nothing to be ashamed of in calling it by its right name!

... HID UNDER THE TABLE AND MADE RUDE NOISES ...

Four

OUR CHILDREN – RIGHT OR WRONG

The reason for children's good manners

Good manners begin in a good home.

The teaching of good manners is the earliest stage of a child's education. Usually the first two words a baby learns to say are 'Mummy' and 'Daddy'. Among the next six will be 'please', 'thank you', and 'good-bye'. These three are, of course, simply vocal tokens of good manners.

It amazes me how many parents are most insistent on their young children behaving properly, but have only the slightest regard for their own good manners within the home.

The other day I went to call on a woman whose little boy had been ill. I took him a book as a gift and tried to present it. The child hid under the table and made rude noises when invited to come out.

'He's that strong-willed we can't do anything with him,' the mother smiled. She spoke with pride; her son's bad behaviour was obviously a boastful topic of conversation.

81

'What a pity! I shall have to take this present home with me,' I said.

There was silence from under the table while we talked of other things. When I was ready to go, a voice called:

'I want my present!'

I paid no attention. Finally, when I was actually on the front door step, a somewhat shame-faced figure appeared and demanded his book.

I hoped his mother would scold him, but she merely laughed: 'He's a limb, isn't he? I'm sure I don't know what we'll do when he gets older.'

I was sure of one thing—that boy would grow into a difficult, uncontrollable adolescent; he might even become a juvenile delinquent, and it will not be his fault.

Of all examples of misguided kindness this sort of lack of parental control is the worst. Good behaviour is not an instinct. The child who receives no training in etiquette and good manners will grow up a primitive savage and an intolerable bore. Perhaps the parents are ready to endure the miseries they inflict on themselves for the sake of avoiding infantile repressions—the inevitable excuse born of a little dangerous knowledge of psychology— but it is extremely unfair on the children.

Three years ago when I was visiting a Council School and being taken round by the Head-

A DOZEN BOYS WERE LOLLING ABOUT

master, we entered a classroom where fully a dozen boys were lolling about, apparently doing nothing.

The Headmaster spoke to one and he answered in an off-hand manner, not bothering even to straighten himself.

When we got outside I asked:

'Don't your boys stand up when you speak to them and call you "Sir"?'

'Good heavens, no,' he answered. 'All that nonsense is a relic of feudalism when village children touched their forelock and said "Good morning, Vicar". Nowadays, children instinctively have good manners.'

'I don't agree,' I said. 'I've never met a child who was born house-trained.'

He looked surprised and I went on:

'What is more, I'm terribly sorry for your boys when they do their National Service. They won't have a chance of advancement or of ever getting a commission because they will be in competition with boys from public and private schools who have all been taught the discipline of good manners as a matter of course.'

When I left the school, I left behind a silent and rather thoughtful Headmaster.

Security is the word every parent and every schoolmaster should bear in mind. Life is a pretty complicated business for us; for a child it is sometimes terrifyingly so. He needs discipline, firmness and possibly punishment, to indicate the right road. How to behave cannot be left to his intelligence. Much of our behaviour is, on first analysis, without rhyme and with little reason. Yet a child quickly discovers that good behaviour is a means of living pleasantly, so that the more he is taught about the rules, the happier he will be.

A politician, now rising to Ministerial heights, was brought up by his parents to 'express himself'.

'Looking back now, I realise how much I disliked being "free",' he told me. 'I used to be rude deliberately to see what my father's guests would do. Their shocked faces and tightened lips used to make me feel ashamed, although I would never have admitted it. My own children are being brought up kindly, but strictly.'

I remember, too, a very charming woman slapping her small son who was showing off, and saying firmly:

'If anyone is going to be temperamental in this house, it will be me!'

Her children are models of good behaviour and everyone likes them.

Children's speech

Constant correction of a child's speech is to be avoided. A veto on words and phrases may merely make them the more intriguing.

The use of 'baby words' is a problem. Some speech therapists deprecate the use of such words as 'ta' for 'thank you' and 'bye-byes' for 'sleep' because they have to be un-learned later.

I feel that this is much too pedantic. An expression of gratitude is the first piece of etiquette a child will be taught. Unfortunately 'thank you' is difficult. 'Ta' is a much simpler word. It is better to say 'ta' than nothing at all. At the age of four or five 'ta' will be forgotten and 'thank you' will become normal.

Christian names and nicknames

Nicknames and diminutives of Christian names should be avoided as they are often ridiculous when one is grown up. I deliberately chose names for my three children which could not be corrupted into diminutives. It is impossible to shorten Raine, Ian or Glen.

It is worth parents' while to think seriously about Christian names when they are choosing them. The psychological, as well as the social, effects of Christian names in later life are rarely taken into account.

For instance Viscount Lymington told me how he suffered at school. His family name was Wallop, and his parents, with what appears to be an almost incredible insensitivity, christened him Oliver Kintzing. His schoolmates could not resist the obvious invitation of

'O. K. Wallop'.

Names should be used by children when talking to others. 'Yes Mummy', 'No, thank you, Mrs Jones', 'Hallo, Aunt Jane' are obviously better manners than 'Yes', 'No, thank you', and 'Hallo'.

Boys should be taught at a very early age—six or seven—to say 'Sir' to an older man. They will continue to do this until they are about twenty-one. Even then, distinguished personages are always referred to with this courtesy.

It should not be embarrassingly repetitive. 'How do you do, Sir' when the boy is introduced, is correct; and 'Sir' should be added in conversation when addressing the older man direct: 'Don't you think so, Sir?'

Children should be encouraged to voice their opinions. But they are entitled to hear sensible, simple arguments on why they are wrong, their views at the same time being taken seriously and not laughed at. Children should never be allowed to contradict without being encouraged to explain why they do so.

Playmates

When children become old enough to form friendships, they face their first problem of social intercourse. They are almost certain to get to know children who, by adult standards, are not suitable companions.

It is a difficult task, too, for a parent to encourage one friendship or stifle another. In the first place the child will feel great pride in deciding on a social activity which is outside his family— one of the first purely social moves he makes of his own accord. He will usually be extremely definite about his decision, and he can rarely

CHILDREN WHO ARE NOT SUITABLE COMPANIONS

be forced to like some friend chosen by his parents or ordered to stop liking one they consider unsuitable.

I remember telling my son Ian to ask to tea a certain little girl whom he met in the Park.

'Mrs X is a great friend of mine and so charming,' I said.

'But we've got to ask her daughter, not her,' Ian replied gloomily with unshakeable logic.

The only thing to do is to guide friendships with discretion and even guile. The criterion should be the character of the other child, and probably of his parents too; never of the social or economic position.

My mother was very wise when my brothers first started to bring home their girl friends. She never criticised or abused the girl. If she was unsuitable, my mother merely said:

'Of course, she's charming, darling—but do you really think she is good enough for you?'

It was extraordinary how those girls melted away like a mist!

In the congested urban and suburban areas in which most people in Britain live, with a cross-section of every class cheek-by-jowl, it is absolutely inevitable that all children will have friends in a different stratum of life from themselves. They will probably meet at school, in children's religious activities, and later, in youth organisations like the Scouts and Guides.

It is absolutely right that they should do so.

No better education for tolerant and well-mannered living can be hoped for than that a child should learn early in life to be a good mixer.

Small children also usually have much more idea than we might expect about differences in social behaviour.

I remember my younger son becoming very attached, during the war, to a small boy who had been evacuated to our village and who used the most appalling language. When I heard Glen swearing, I told him it was wrong.

'Ivor says that,' he replied.

'Ivor doesn't know any better,' I replied; 'but you do.'

He considered this for some time.

'I expect Ivor's Mummy doesn't know any better,' he said, 'so we won't tell him it's wrong.'

It was an example of tact which no diplomat could have bettered.

Education

Ignorance is a degrading form of servitude. Education's purpose is to make a young person free and to permit him to take his place in society in order to benefit both it and himself.

Education should not be expected to cram facts into the mind, but to encourage the use of faculties which are dormant.

Stanley Baldwin said that 'the difference

between a man of intellect and an intellectual is roughly the same as between a gentleman and a gent.' It is worth remembering that the well bred and educated man is not always advertising the fact, whereas the badly bred and half educated man will be constantly exhibiting his learning or lack of it.

When selecting a school for a child, neither the buildings, nor the record of examination passes, nor the names of notabilities who attended in the past matter. The only factors to study are the traditional spirit of the place and the characters of the teaching staff.

As a member of the Hertfordshire Education Committee I visit numbers of schools and I have also lectured in a great many in Canada. I can tell as soon as I meet the Head Master or Mistress what the school is like.

It was the Queen Mother who said 'Reforms come from the top'. In schools, not only reforms, but examples, atmosphere and incentive come from the top. There is, in my opinion, no more important position today for a man or a woman than that of guiding and inspiring a new generation.

Good manners are an essential in every school, and where the Head believes in courtesy, consideration and kindliness, then the boys and girls he teaches will come not only to believe in them, but to practise them.

Children and guests

'I used to enjoy visiting John and Mary,' a neighbour said to me about a mutual acquaintance. 'John is an old political adversary of mine and we had a lot of interest in arguing about agreeing to differ. And my wife got on well with Mary: the usual sort of women's gossip. But now, well, half the evening's spent in smoothing down childish tantrums and trying to keep the conversation going at a level they can understand so they don't make a scene.'

John and Mary have twins, now eleven years old. Their parents worship them, and spoil them. That is their own affair, but unfortunately they inflict the bad results on their guests.

In most houses today children have to be in the living-room until their bedtime. It is a pity that we do not adopt the American and Canadian idea of a 'rumpus room', usually in the basement below the house, which takes up no more building area and adds very little to the original building cost. It is even more of a pity that parents do not face earlier the problem which confronts them when a child is in its teens—that the bedroom shall also be a sitting-room.

Apart from the fact that the child deserves and needs privacy this overcomes the problem of ill-assorted age groups when guests are entertained.

On informal guest occasions, children who would normally have an evening meal may be allowed to have dinner. They should then be old enough to obey previously-given instructions to disappear after a quietly spoken good-night before coffee is served. Younger children, if it is at all possible, should be in bed before the guests arrive. This can be arranged either by advancing the bedtime a little or delaying the appointed time of the guests' arrival.

All children, unless the guests are relatives or very close friends, should be out of the way for formal evening occasions.

Most embarrassing of all is the spoiled child who is shown off by the over-proud parents. Even people who love children do not want to sit transfixed with a beatific smile on their faces while little Dottie sings her song or little Tim recites his version of a couple of dozen nursery rhymes.

Being in the limelight invariably causes young children to be shy at first, and then having been cajoled to strut on the stage and do their party piece the whole business is likely to go to their heads and there are tears and temper when the parents call a halt.

Just as children have their own parties when adults are not expected to attend, except as helpers, so children should be taught from the beginning that within the framework of family life there are occasions when the parents entertain friends. If the awful temptation to show off the infant who is just lisping its first words or taking its hesitant steps is resisted, then this occasional phase of 'adults only' will be accepted without any question—and probably with relief.

At the same time the other extreme is to be regretted. I know a young man who lost the chance of quick promotion to managership of a branch of his employer's firm in this way.

His managing director, anxious to know something of his employee's private life and

THE SPOILED CHILD WHO IS SHOWN OFF

personal attitudes for a post where social stability as represented by a happy marriage and a sense of family responsibilities would be essential, got himself invited to dinner.

The young man, who suspected that promotion was possible, became vastly excited. His wife, a charming and intelligent girl, was delighted to help by planning a simple but well cooked meal.

Positive that his boss would want to talk business from the moment he came till he left, and knowing him only as the rather severe and serious business man of office hours, the young husband persuaded his wife to send their five-year-old son to relatives for the night.

The result was that when the managing director asked about the child he got a terse, 'Oh, he's staying with his aunt and uncle just now,' from the husband, and a mumbled 'young children can be such a nuisance,' from the wife.

Quite erroneously the guest decided that the child was unwanted and that there was some kind of tension between husband and wife. He made up his mind then and there that the marriage was heading for disaster.

As a matter of fact, that elderly business man would have loved to have carried the boy piggy-back to bed just as he did his own grandchildren. He would have been impressed with the cleanliness, good behaviour and politeness of an extremely well-brought-up and dearly loved child.

Possibly not all adults like children in that way, but none worth knowing resents being politely greeted by a child, either by 'Miss—' or 'Mrs—' or, in the case of men, by 'Sir'.

If your children are badly behaved then keep them away from your guests, thereby admitting frankly that you are a failure as a parent. It is better that way than to prove it by scenes.

If they have been properly disciplined then allow your children briefly to meet your guests, for when they visit your home they are meeting you in your private life, and the children are as much part of it as a wife or husband.

But don't risk the chance of having to rebuke or punish your children before guests. It is embarrassing for the visitor, galling for you and degrading for the child. The last is the only one who will have the bravado to indicate how he feels by showing off in an outburst of temper which will merely aggravate an already awkward moment.

If, however, you are guest in a house where a child is punished or rebuked in front of you, do not interfere, however badly you want to. Things have probably gone too far for you to placate the child, and if you add your own reprimand you will arouse the parent's indignation. Try to do the impossible by ignoring the

whole thing and rapidly change the subject
once the erring child has been dragged, screaming and protesting, to its bedroom.

... ERRING CHILD DRAGGED OFF KICKING AND
SCREAMING

97

Dress

Cleanliness and simplicity are two desirable factors in children's dress. A third is timeliness.

Children get grubby, but it is never too early to teach them that they must wash their hands before meals, after going to the lavatory and before going to bed. They must also learn early in life to change muddy shoes on coming into the house and to hang up their own coats and hats.

Simplicity is necessary because a child is a simple person. Doting mothers who put too many frills and furbelows on their children's clothing are not only embarrassing the child, but exhibiting their own lack of good taste.

Timeliness may seem a curious thing to consider. But parents have a habit of wanting to put the hands of the clock forward or back. Perhaps a mother wants her baby to remain the cuddlesome, helpless thing she loved in his first two years. Subconsciously she retains baby clothes and baby hair styles too long. Or perhaps she longs to see her son a man, so she puts him into long trousers years before they are necessary.

In the early teens or just before, both boys and girls may have a bizarre taste in clothes. Here a gentle and inconspicuous guiding hand is needed. Party dress for a boy is a plain navy suit. If and when he goes to a well-known public school he should have a dinner jacket, otherwise a navy suit will serve him until he is eighteen.

Make-up

Make-up for young girls should, of course, be used with discretion but every mother is involved in the same battle with daughters between the ages of twelve and sixteen.

I always advise mothers to take their daughters to a Beauty Parlour and have them shown how to make-up properly.

It is the experiments which are so painful and expensive and it's no use expecting that a modern girl won't want to make-up as soon as she reaches puberty—because she will.

The great thing is to see that a standard of good taste in lipstick and eyeshade is reached as quickly as possible. The cost is not exorbitant and in practically every provincial town today it is possible to find an expert to advise young girls on the care of their skin and hair.

Addressing adults

'Mummy' and 'Daddy' have become universal terms among all classes of children when addressing their parents.

It is not a serious solecism to shorten Daddy to Dad, but Mum is a term to avoid. Ma and Pa are obviously abhorrent, but it is noteworthy that our present Queen and Princess Margaret always addressed their father as Papa from their babyhood until the King died. Mama is seldom heard these days.

Modes of address of uncles and aunts, cousins and second cousins, present no problems. The basically incorrect use of 'uncle' and 'aunt' for older cousins and adult in-laws is acceptable by general usage and many close friends of the family are addressed in the same way.

Children should never be allowed to address servants, tradesmen or employees by surname only, even though their parents do.

Children's letters

Letter writing is rapidly becoming a lost art, which is all the more reason to encourage children to practise it. Everyone appreciates a letter of thanks and children should always write to thank for gifts, parties and holidays.

My children started this duty at the age of four or five. At the same age I remember weeping bitter tears at the hated desk, but the discipline was well worth the cost because today I find letters of thanks are easy to write and to express.

It is important older children should write naturally in their own words. But it is wise to 'vet' the letters after they have finished them.

The form of a thank you letter is as important for children as it is for grown-ups. The 'thanks' must come at the beginning *and* at the end. Here is an example.

December 31st. 1961

My dear Aunt Grace,

Thank you so very much for the lovely box of soldiers you sent me for Christmas. It is exactly what I wanted and John and I have had great fun playing with them.

Again thank you a thousand times for the wonderful present.

Love from your affectionate nephew,

Alan.

Children should also be instructed in the correct form of address and ending. 'Lots of love from...' or 'Yours affectionately' is the usual ending for all children's letters.

Letters to boys from adults should be addressed 'Master John Jones' or simply 'John Jones' until the boy is eighteen. If, however, he goes to a public school it is correct to put 'John Jones, Esq.'

Children have to be taught to be demonstrative and should not write 'Dear Mummy'. As I said to my children when they tried it: 'I am not a shop.'

The usual rule is:

'Darling Mummy and Daddy,' to their parents.

'Dearest or Darling Granny and Grandpa,' to their grandparents.

'My dear Uncle and Aunt,'

'Dear Mr X,' to all other persons.

Five

INVITATIONS

There are many formal rules for the sending and answering of invitations. I am therefore showing as clearly as possible the form an invitation should take for some particular function and the correct way of accepting or refusing it.

All invitations should be engraved in copperplate writing where it can be afforded. Where this comes too expensive, they should be printed to look as much like engraving as possible.

Invitations must always be in black on a white card or folder with a plain edge. All elaborations of gold, silver, fluted edges or antique paper are incorrect.

Wedding invitations

Let us first look at wedding invitations. These are engraved or printed on a double sheet of paper using only the front sheet. The guest's name is written by hand in the top left-hand corner *(See page 114)*.

The reply is written by hand —not typed— and should be as follows:

Mr and Mrs Hugh McCorquodale have much pleasure in accepting the kind invitation of

Brigadier and Mrs. Hanbury to the marriage of their daughter Penelope at St. James's, Spanish Place, on Thursday April 2nd., and afterwards at The Hyde Park Hotel.

The envelope should be addressed to Mrs Hanbury at Hay Lodge, Braughing, Ware, Herts.

A refusal should read:

Mr and Mrs Hugh McCorquodale regret they cannot accept the kind invitation of Brigadier and Mrs. Hanbury to the marriage of their daughter on Thursday, April 2nd., owing to a previous engagement.

Both these replies are shorter than would have been considered etiquette twenty-five years ago, but they are correct for today.

Where a marriage has been dissolved and the mother of the bride has married again, the invitation should then read:

Mr Charles Smith and Mrs Douglas Robinson
request the pleasure of
your company at the marriage of
their daughter
Sarah Jane
etc.

Dinner invitations

Most dinner parties are arranged over the telephone or the hostess writes a personal letter of invitation. For very formal occasions a card may be sent *(See page 117)*.

The guest's name is written in the top left hand corner by hand and this formula is the same for Dances and Cocktail Parties, the only alteration being in the bottom right-hand corner. For cocktail parties it is usual to put 6.30 to 8.30, or whatever time you expect your guests.

For ordinary dinner parties and for informal dances you can also put 'Black Tie' in the bottom right-hand corner. If this is not there, then the men are expected to wear tails.

So many people give informal parties nowadays when men come straight on from the office without changing that it is always wise to telephone and ask what everyone will be wearing. The same applies for women.

At most dinner parties at which the men wear a dinner jacket the ladies wear short dresses, but nothing is more embarrassing than to arrive and find oneself the only guest in a short dress or evening dress, as the case may be.

There need be no embarrassment in asking. If the party is a charity event or given by an organisation, telephone the secretary. If it is a private occasion and a member of the staff answers your telephone call, you can ask him or her what the host and hostess will be wearing.

Invitations to a Dance, a Buffet Luncheon and a Cocktail Party are shown on pages 116, 118 and 119.

Replies are written in the third person and you do not put 'At Home'. The right formula is:

Mr and Mrs Hugh McCorquodale have much pleasure in accepting the kind invitation of Lady Aldenham for Sunday, May 10th. at 6 o'clock.

Civic invitations

Civic invitations are worded rather differently and the names are written in the centre of the card *(See page 115)*.

Reminders

Many people send a reminder if their guests have been invited a week or two in advance. This is usually on a postcard, but can be printed as the one on page 114.

A more ordinary reminder on normal writing paper or a postcard, reads:

Mrs Hugh McCorquodale is very much looking forward to seeing you for dinner at 8 o'clock on Tuesday, May 2nd. Black tie.

People who entertain a lot, but for quite small parties often have a card engraved *(See page 119)*.

This means they only have to fill in the date, time and type of party. An even cheaper

...THE ONLY GUEST IN A SHORT DRESS

method is to buy 'At Home' cards at any stationer. These are the correct shape but contain the words 'At Home' and 'R.S.V.P.' and you fill in the rest.

Answering invitations

All invitations are answered exactly in the same way in which they are written—the details of the invitation being quoted. Refusals always say: 'Owing to another engagement', unless one is away from home and then one can say: '....as they will be away from home on that date.'

Invitations should be answered, if possible, by return. Nothing is more annoying than guests who wait until the last moment before saying yes or no.

Weekends

Invitations to acquaintances for the weekend should contain all the important details they will want to know about your household. Many people entertain overseas business visitors who are absolutely mystified as to when to arrive, what to wear and when to leave unless it is put clearly in a letter.

The hostess always writes a letter of invitation, addressing herself to the wife if a married couple are being invited. Here is an example in which every detail is included:

Dear Mrs Wallis,

We would be so delighted if you and your husband could come and stay with us next weekend, Friday, May 15th. until Monday, May 18th. There is a good train leaving Victoria at 5.30 p.m. which arrives at Copperfield at 6.20 p.m. where I would meet you; or if you come by car, I will send you a route.

We will have a few friends to meet you on Saturday evening and John is longing for a round of golf with your husband on Saturday afternoon. On Sunday, if the weather is fine, we will play tennis, so do bring your rackets.

We are so looking forward to seeing you both and if you want a lift up to London on Monday morning I could take you both with me as I have to be at my dentist's at eleven o'clock.

With all best wishes,
Yours sincerely,

Omitted invitations

It is never, never correct to ask for an invitation, but any organiser of a big social event will know that many and varied are the ingenious methods in which 'gate-crashers' attempt to obtain invitations.

You may hear of some local occasion to which you believe that you are so obviously entitled to be invited that your name has been omitted in error or the invitation has been lost in the post.

No matter if you have been invited on every occasion in the past and if you know beyond all doubt that everyone expects that you will be there, there is nothing that you should do personally or through a third party.

The mistake, if it is a mistake, will probably be discovered at the eleventh hour when you can show your breeding by being magnanimous. If there is no mistake, the insult, real or imagined, will fail to register if you maintain a quiet dignity and ignore the whole thing.

Invitations to newcomers

Leaving visiting cards with new people who have arrived in the neighbourhood in which you live is completely out of date. No one has time for it. But somehow one has to get to know new arrivals and if you live in London you will often be asked to 'be kind' to a friend of a friend. It is always the duty of the one who was there first to make the overtures of friendliness. What is usual is for the established resident to write:

Dear Mrs Brown,

I was so interested to learn that you and your husband have come to live in Little Bankwell. I hope you will forgive me for not calling on you as at the moment I am overwhelmed with work but it would be delightful if you and your husband would come in for a drink next

Saturday at 6.30. We will so look forward to seeing you and I do hope you will be very happy in your new home.

Yours sincerely,

Most people scribble their signatures so when writing letters of this sort it is wise to print your name, with any prefix you may have, in capitals, above the address.

Note. It is wrong to sign your letters: '(Mrs) Alice Bloggs'. And it is also wrong to sign letters with only your initials. I am always getting letters signed 'A.D.Smith'. How am I to know if it is Mr, Mrs or Miss?

LETTERS WHICH WON'T OFFEND

The telephone has almost killed the art of letter writing, which is a pity because both sending and receiving letters can give infinitely more pleasure than speaking on the telephone.

Writing a letter obviously involves much more trouble than lifting a receiver, and for that reason a letter is a symbol of good manners to a greater extent than just ringing someone up.

Letter writing, however, is an art which has to be cultivated, for different styles are needed for different letters. It should be perfectly obvious that the manner of writing to a favourite aunt is very different from that to a distant friend, or a letter to a tradesman from that to a bank manager.

Writing paper and envelopes

First impressions are of enormous importance and so it is as well to consider the kind of writing paper which is appropriate. Incidentally to say '*note* paper' is incorrect. The old-fashioned idea was for all private correspondence to be written on thick paper folded down the middle so that it made a piece of four pages.

Most people nowadays use single sheets of paper made in a block for convenience. But if a four-page type of writing paper is used, it is correct to start the letter on the first page and continue on the back of the first page and straight on.

Headings

The address should be engraved in the right-hand corner or centre of the paper and should be in black with the plainest possible lettering.

Crests

Crests are permissible if one is entitled to one, but monograms, initials and arty-crafty designs for the address are completely wrong.

The Queen has the Royal Coat of Arms in the centre of her writing paper with BUCKINGHAM PALACE in very plain lettering underneath, but all in red. Colours are, however, for most people inadvisable.

BEGINNING A LETTER

Brigadier and Mrs. Richard Hanbury
request the pleasure of
your company at the marriage
of their daughter
Penelope
to
Mr. John Nugent
at St. James's, Spanish Place,
on Thursday, April 2nd,
at 4 o'clock
and afterwards at
The Hyde Park Hotel

R.S.V.P.
Hay Lodge,
Braughing,
Ware, Herts.

A WEDDING INVITATION

The Corporation of London
requests the pleasure of the Company of

at Guildhall on Monday, the 17th March, 1958
at 8 p.m.
at a Reception in honour of
Her Majesty Queen Elizabeth the Queen Mother.

R.S.V.P. to
The Town Clerk
Guildhall, E.C.2

Evening Dress with Decorations

Carriages at 11 p.m.

THIS CARD WILL NOT ADMIT

AN INVITATION TO A RECEPTION

115

Countess of Cottenham

at Home

Tuesday, 19th May

at The Dorchester

(Ballroom Entrance)

R.S.V.P.   *Dancing 10.30 o'clock.*
Hungerhill House,   *Black Tie*
Coolham, Sussex.

PLEASE BRING THIS INVITATION WITH YOU

AN INVITATION TO A DANCE

The Italian Ambassador

requests the pleasure of

Company at

4, Grosvenor Square, W.1   *To remind*

A REMINDER

The Netherlands Ambassador
and Baroness Bentinck

request the pleasure of the company of

on   at   o'clock

R.S.V.P.

Netherlands Embassy
8 Palace Green, W.8

AN INVITATION TO A DINNER PARTY

Mrs. John Coats and Mrs. Hervey-Bathurst

Mary Manuela and Selena

At Home

Monday 25th April

Buffet Luncheon at the River Room, Savoy Hotel

Savoy Embankment Entrance

R.S.V.P

15 Markham Square,
S.W.3

1 - 3 p.m

AN INVITATION TO A BUFFET LUNCHEON

Mrs. Hugh McCorquodale

At Home

_____

R.S.V.P.
Camfield Place
Hatfield

A GENERAL INVITATION CARD

Lady Aldenton

at Home

Cocktails
6:30 -8:30 pm

R.S.V.P.
Belton House
Ware

AN INVITATION TO A COCKTAIL PARTY

Mrs. Hugh McCorquodale

Camfield Place,
Hatfield, Hertfordshire

Mrs. Hugh McCorquodale

Camfield Place,
Hatfield, Hertfordshire

VISITING CARDS

120

Beginning a letter

The beginning and ending of letters can give rise to mistakes. On page 127 there is a list of the correct forms of address to persons of rank, the clergy and so on, and these must be followed exactly.

Writing your name

When writing to a stranger about selling your house, buying something that is advertised etc., always start, 'Dear Sir' or 'Dear Madam'. If there is no name to denote sex, 'Dear Sir or Madam'.

Do write your own name in block capitals above the address. I go nearly mad trying to decipher signatures which look as if a drunken spider had walked over the page.

I also find it very difficult to guess who 'Betty', 'Joan' or 'Mary' is who writes to me from some holiday resort. I know two or three dozen women with those Christian names.

Unless you know anyone very well indeed, when you are away from home, always add a surname even to your close friends.

Christian names

Never call a public person whom you don't know by their Christian name in a letter. I think it awful cheek if—as many people do—

someone I have never met writes to me 'Dear Barbara'. I don't like 'Dear Barbara Cartland' either. 'Dear Miss Cartland' is correct.

Ending a letter

The conclusion of a letter should be 'Yours truly' to a shop and in the case of most business letters. 'Yours sincerely' is for social letters. 'Yours affectionately', 'Yours ever' and similar terms are for letters of an intimate nature. It is wrong to say 'Sincerely yours' or 'Ever yours'. Except in very formal letters additions to the final phrase, such as 'I remain', 'Believe me', should not be used.

Sir and Madam

Letters should rarely, if ever, begin 'Sir' or 'Madam'. Obviously such letters are only written for the conduct of some quarrel and dispute. They smack of a missive from a solicitor and if they have to be written it is probably safer that somebody with legal training should write them.

There do, unfortunately, have to be letters which are, to all intents and purposes, threats, but it is undesirable that a lay person should risk being unnecessarily rude, quite apart from the dangers of legal action which this sort of letter can involve.

Signatures

Never under any circumstances sign your letter Mr and Mrs—even in brackets. Put your full name over the address, or if you prefer it, sign your letter 'Mary Jones' and write formally in block capitals 'MRS TOM JONES'.

Married woman's name

Always remember that you take your husband's name if you are married, except on election lists. The rules are:

1. Unmarried woman—Miss Mary Brown.
2. When she marries she becomes Mrs Tom Jones.
3. A woman whose marriage has been dissolved and whose husband has married again is—Mrs Mary Jones.

In the event of someone having a title the rule is:

1. Married woman—Lady Robinson.
2. If marriage is dissolved and Sir John Robinson marries again, she becomes—Jean, Lady Robinson.

First or third person

The old-time conception of writing was that a note was written in the third person and a letter in the first person.

If you write a letter saying: 'Mrs Jones has pleasure in enclosing a cheque for five pounds in settlement of the attached account', you, of course, do not add your signature.

Phrasing letters

As regards the phraseology used in letters the great thing is to be as brief as possible and as natural.

Few correspondents will find it difficult to write naturally to people they know well, but

BE AS BRIEF AS POSSIBLE

many resort to the most peculiar words and phrases when penning a formal letter.

The imitation of the all too common style of the letter from a business concern is to be deprecated. 'I am in receipt of your esteemed communication of the 20th. inst.' is an absurd way of saying 'I was glad to get your letter of the 20th.'

Abbreviations.

The closer one writes a letter to the style in which one would speak in person or over the telephone, the better; but except in very informal letters it is undesirable to use abbreviations and elisions. Thus one should write 'I am' although one would say 'I'm'.

Postscripts

Postscripts are sometimes inevitable although they tend to suggest a certain carelessness in composing the letter in that something one wishes to say was forgotten until the end or until reading the letter over.

But over the years the postscript has so often been possibly the most urgent piece of information in the whole letter that it is now accepted as a means of accentuating something important.

It is not today regarded as necessary to write the letters P.S. The additional sentence is simply added below the signature.

Addressing the envelope

There are a great many formalities about the addressing of envelopes. For example, the majority of men addressed as Colonel are, in fact, Lieutenant Colonels, so that the envelope would bear the words: Lieutenant Colonel J. J. Smith. The letter would start "Dear Colonel Smith".

The same distinction applies in the case of the majority of Generals who are, in fact, Major-Generals or Lieutenant-Generals.

An important exception to remember in the case of officers of the Armed Services is that a Lieutenant or Sub-Lieutenant in the Royal Navy or a First- or Second-Lieutenant in the Army have no rank in social life. The name on the envelope must therefore not give the rank but simply the names followed by Esq.

The use of Esq.

The use of Esq. is today universal, although originally it implied a social position of some importance. The rule to follow today is that Esq. can always be used instead of Mr. It is, however, wrong to address an envelope to a person in Holy Orders, a doctor, a professor and so on by omitting his prefix title and using Esq.

Clergy

A Parson is addressed as the Rev. John Smith.

A Canon is addressed as Canon John Smith.

A Dean is addressed as The Very Reverend the Dean of —.

An Archdeacon is addressed as The Venerable the Archdeacon of —.

A Bishop is addressed as The Right Rev. the Lord Bishop of —.

Retired Bishops are addressed as The Right Rev. Bishop —.

An Archbishop is addressed as His Grace Lord Archbishop of —.

Judges

A Judge is addressed as Hon. Mr Justice —. On the Bench he is spoken to as 'My Lord'.

A Judge of a County Court is addressed as His Honour Judge —. On the Bench he is spoken to as 'Your Honour'.

A Commonwealth Judge is addressed as Hon. AB or Hon. Mr Justice —.

Mayors

A Mayor is addressed as The Right Worshipful the Mayor of —.

A Lord Mayor is addressed as The Right Worshipful the Lord Mayor of —.

The Lord Mayors of London, York, Belfast, Sydney, Melbourne, Adelaide, Perth,

Brisbane and Hobart are addressed as The Right Hon. Lord Mayor of —.

The Lord Mayor's wife is addressed as The Lady Mayoress.

Titled persons

The following is the correct way to address titled persons with whom you have an acquaintance. For a more formal approach see Debrett.

On an envelope

A Duke	The Duke of X
A Marquis	The Marquis of X
An Earl	The Earl of X
A Viscount	Viscount X
A Baron	The Lord X
A Baronet	Sir Hugh L... Bt.
A Knight	Sir Ian K...
Dames	Dame Alice... D.B.E.

	In a letter	In conversation
A Duke	My dear Duke	Duke
A Marquis	Dear Lord X	Lord X
An Earl	Dear Lord X	Lord X
A Viscount	Dear Lord X	Lord X
A Baron	Dear Lord X	Lord X
A Baronet	Dear Sir Hugh	Sir Hugh
A Knight	Dear Sir Ian	Sir Ian
Dames	Dear Dame Alice	Dame Alice

Servants address of titles

Note: Servants call Dukes, 'His Grace' or 'Your Grace'; Marquises, Earls, Viscounts and Barons 'm' Lord'; Baronets, 'Sir Hugh' (or whatever his Christian name is); Knights, 'Sir'. Dames are called 'm' Lady'.

Honourables

Honourables are the younger sons of Marquises and Earls, and the sons and daughters of Barons. A letter to one of them starts, 'Dear Mr X' or 'Dear Miss X', but on the envelope should be written, 'The Honourable Gerald X' or 'The Honourable Alice X'.

It is not correct to put 'The Hon.' but so many people do it to save time and space that it has become acceptable.

Honourables are never introduced as such; in fact almost the only time they use their title is on an envelope. But be very careful, at dinner parties they come quite high in order of precedence.

Honours and decorations

Writers of letters should always be very careful to put after a man's name the initials which denote his position such as, J.P. (Justice of the Peace) and his decorations. The following is the right order for the best known British decorations:

V.C. (Victoria Cross), G.C. (George Cross), O.M. (Order of Merit), C.I. (cross of India), C.H. (Companion of Honour), C.B. (Commander of the Bath), C.S.I. (Commander of the Star of India), C.M.G. (Commander of the Order of St. Michael and St. George), C.I.E. (Commander of the Indian Empire), C.V.O. (Commander of the Victorian Order), C.B.E. (Commander of the British Empire), D.S.O. (Distinguished Service Order), M.V.O. (Member of the Victorian Order), O.B.E. (Order of the British Empire), M.B.E. (Member of the British Empire), R.R.C. (Royal Red Cross), D.S.C. (Distinguished Service Cross), M. C. (Military Cross), D.F.C. (Distinguished Flying Cross).

Knights start with: K.B.E. (Knight Commander of the British Empire), K.C.V.O. (Knight Commander of the Victorian Order), K.C.I.E. (Knight Commander of the Indian Empire), K.C.M.G. (Knight Commander of St. Michael and St. George), K.C.S.I. (Knight Commander of the Star of India) and K.C.B. (Knight Commander of the Bath).

Privy Councillors: The courtesy title of Right Honourable is accorded to all Privy Councillors and the office is conferred for life. Wives do not share this title. On an envelope you put, "The Rt Hon. James Blank, P.C., M.P."

Other distinctions

For Members of Parliament put M.P. after their name. Queen's Councillors—Q.C.; Justices of the Peace—J.C.; County Councillors—C.C.; London County Councillors—L.C.C.; Surgeons, who are addressed as Esq. not as Doctor, have F.R.C.S. after their Esq. (Fellow of the Royal College of Surgeons).

One or two names

The old rule was that no envelope should bear more than one name because only one person can open a letter. Invitations should always go to the wife even if you are personally acquainted with only the husband, for a wife is, in effect, the arbiter of the social activities of the marriage. Note, too, that it is very rude to ask a husband to anything but a 'stag party' without his wife.

Christmas cards

In recent times Christmas cards have been sent in increasing numbers, but that is no excuse for the lazy and rude habit of having them printed 'from Mr and Mrs X'.

The Queen and all members of the Royal Family sign their Christmas cards personally. If you don't know a person well enough to sign your Christmas card don't send him one. This applies to the personal card sent privately.

There are business and professional men who may send hundreds, or even thousands, of cards and in this case it is acceptable to have the card printed with a facsimile signature.

On the vexed question of what card to send, when to send it, and to whom, some thought is necessary. Snobbery and status-seeking has unfortunately crept into a custom connected with a festival symbolising the very reverse of these worldly things. 'The bigger the card the better the impression' seems to be the policy of some people; others select cards for their novelty value. Both types probably offend as many recipients as they impress or please.

It is worth remembering that for most people Christmas cards are something to be used as a Christmas decoration. Therefore a card which carries a friendly greeting and looks attractive, should be selected.

Although I feel that the great festival of the Christian year should certainly have some part in the picture on a Christmas card, it should be remembered that among one's friends there may be those of the Jewish faith who, while they enjoy the secular side of Christmas and love to receive greetings cards, could be offended by receiving pictures of the Nativity.

Equally, the licence given to artists to caricature the shepherds, the manger scene, and other characters and incidents of the Bible story, can offend some deeply devout persons.

132

If we must avoid the toil of writing personal greetings notes by buying greetings cards we can at least have the sensitivity to choose cards appropriate to our friends. The religious belief, age, and intimacy of the recipient of each card should be considered.

It is virtually impossible to find a standard greeting suitable for all even if the illustration is suitable. Older relatives, who study the words meticulously, can be hurt when they get a card which states coldly and formally 'Season's Greetings from...', and one's lawyer or doctor will raise a quizzical eyebrow on reading some bad and highly sentimental verse expressing 'love and hearty wishes for a lot of jolly fun'.

The better firms offer to print cards with a range of greetings as well as the sender's address. It is socially acceptable—and probably desirable—to have your address printed, but to omit the name. Then you can add a few personal words and sign the card according to your degree of intimacy with the recipient.

Of growing popularity are the cards produced by welfare organisations like the United Nations Children's Fund, the Save the Children Fund, the Oxford Committee for Famine Relief and so on. Most charitable organisations, in fact, sell their own Christmas cards. They improve every year and the range is wide—some are elaborate and expensive and

133

others extremely cheap.

I suggest that no one can possibly go wrong by confining his selection to these cards which solve the purchasing problem, help a good cause, and point out that Christmas is a time of charity and giving, all at the same time.

Whom to send cards to is always a difficult problem. Methodical and cold-hearted people I know keep a list of persons from whom they received cards the previous year and send only to them.

I feel that, having sent a card once, it is kind to continue even if no card was received in return. There may be all sorts of reasons why the card did not arrive, but there can be only one reason for you to decide not to send one—and that is a decision not to want to greet a friend. It is better at all times— and certainly at Christmas— to show friendliness even if you are rebuffed. In any event cards are not sent on a *quid pro quo* basis.

Every year there will be additions to your list. Those nice people you met on holiday, the new family along the road, a recruit to the array of in-laws or prospective in-laws.

I suggest the only rule on whom to include and whom to leave out is to answer the question: 'Do I genuinely want to wish them well?' and, more important: 'Will they be pleased to receive a card from me?'

When you have answered these questions,

send the cards irrespective of whether you are likely to get a card in return.

Short of being psychic there is no possible way of posting cards to reach certain people before theirs reach you. I suggest that posting seven clear weekdays before Christmas Day will nullify any suggestion that you are 'fishing' to get cards in return.

Other 'occasion' cards

The resourceful greetings card industry has produced cards to cover every conceivable occasion and every likely and unlikely relationship! Most of them—birthday cards, Mother's Day cards, wedding anniversary cards—are for use within your intimate family circle.

I think that any recipient would infinitely prefer a handwritten letter, a visit, or a telephone call to the most lavish and expensive of these cards, but if they must be sent, then simplicity and at least a suggestion of sincerity should control the choice. The funny—and particularly 'sick-humour' cards—are not for those who hope never to offend.

It is certainly not etiquette to send any of these cards to neighbours and business acquaintances. Nor is it socially permissible to send the cards produced for such occasions as getting a new job, going on holiday, or celebrating a divorce—all of which are nowadays on sale in the shops.

Letters to sick persons

Least of all is a 'get well soon' card the correct way of expressing sympathy to someone sick at home or ill in hospital. If your emotions are insufficiently stirred to justify the time for a handwritten letter, then it would be best to do nothing at all.

Upon hearing that a friend is ill, enquire if possible from relatives as to the seriousness of the illness. A long, gossipy letter recording one's own sufferings with a similar trouble is undesirable for someone dangerously ill. In such a case a few lines of sympathy and good wishes accompanied by flowers is more appropriate.

If, on the other hand, the trouble is not serious or the patient is getting better, then something to amuse and occupy attention may be welcomed. Remember at all costs that letters to sick people are to express sympathy and goodwill, not to satisfy curiosity. Ask no questions nor make any statement that implies an answer is expected. All questions, if they must be asked, should be through the patient's relatives.

Expressions of sympathy to patients who are mere acquaintances should be expressed verbally or in a brief message to the relative. Social climbers should not use illness to suggest an intimacy which does not exist by ordering large bunches of flowers and baskets of fruit to be sent to the patient's home or hospital.

When you are ill all enquiries, flowers and letters should be acknowledged by a relative as soon as they arrive. And as soon as you are well enough, you must write a letter of thanks yourself.

Charitable appeals

Every week I get about a dozen letters asking me to support dances, premières, bazaars etc., given in aid of some charitable cause. These have a social committee and the letter is supposedly signed by the Chairman. When their signatures are printed I put the appeals straight into the waste paper basket.

Some Chairmen—or should I say, Chairwomen—cheat and have the letters signed by a secretary. I know this when someone who usually addresses me by my Christian name starts 'Dear Miss Cartland'. These letters also go into the waste-paper basket.

A Chairman of any Appeal should word the letter herself in the language she normally uses. The envelope should be addressed by the secretary and the Chairman should 'top and tail' the letter.

Typewritten letters

It used to be rude to write a typewritten letter to a friend. Where there are a lot of explanations to make, and propositions to put forward, a typewritten letter is infinitely preferable to bad writing which is often illegible. Even so it is correct to say, 'Do forgive a typewritten letter'.

A gesture which can add a personal touch to a typewritten letter—and one worth keeping in mind if you do not type the letter yourself—is to hand-write the beginning and end. ('Dear Mr Jones. . . . . . Yours sincerely, Mary Smith').

It is absolutely unforgivable in a letter of a social character—and, to my mind, in a business letter as well— to dictate a letter, have a secretary type it, and tell her to add 'dictated by Mr Jones and signed in his absence by Mary Bloggs'.

No matter how customary it may be to type letters, those of congratulations or condolences must always be written by hand. Also an acceptance or refusal of an invitation.

Letters of introduction

So many people go abroad and so many visit this country from other lands that there is a constant exchange of letters of introduction.

Letters given to a friend by a friend should

never be sealed down. If you want to write something intimate that the person to be introduced should not read, you must send it by post. This is a typical letter of introduction such as I often send:

> Camfield Place,
> Hatfield.
> July 2nd.

Dear Mrs Wasselback,

I am sending you this letter by a great friend of mine, Mrs Donald Blinks, who is paying her first visit to America and will be in New York for three weeks. She is a charming person, young, pretty and gay. Her husband, who is a nephew of Lord Smithers, is a publisher.

It would be so kind if you would invite Diana to your lovely apartment and tell her some of the things she mustn't miss in your exciting city!

Love to you all, and I do hope you will be coming over next autumn.

> Yours affectionately,
> Barbara Cartland.

Business letters of introduction are, of course, worded more formally and give as many details as possible about the person being introduced.

Six

ETIQUETTE FOR HOSTS

'True friendship's laws are by this rule expressed: Welcome the coming, speed the parting guest'.

The thought in this couplet was originally Homer's, and there are few wiser rules for providing hospitality. They summarise the principles of good behaviour between host and guest. But remember that the onus is on the host to make the welcome real.

A dinner party

Nowadays, when few people have any staff, small parties are usually very informal. But the standards of etiquette are still there, so I will describe a dinner party of, say, ten guests given in correct manner with servants, and at the same time show how well you can entertain by doing everything yourself or with the help of your daily woman.

In my opinion ten is a sufficient number for an enjoyable dinner party and in my home we are usually eight. If one is going to talk afterwards, however large the sitting-room, it is difficult to get more than eight people round the fire and keep the conversation general.

The setting of the dinner table is important if a party is to be a success. Tall flowers in the centre prevent people talking across the table and so a flat arrangement is best. The heads of roses, rhododendrons, dahlias or peonies floating in water look lovely.

Also, do decorate your dishes. If I use a glass bowl for my main course or for ice cream I put on the dish upon which it stands flower-heads or leaves according to the season. Such

THE SETTING OF THE DINNER TABLE

an arrangement is always much admired and makes people enjoy their food more.

Americans take a great deal of trouble over the arrangements of their dinner or luncheon table. They have specially coloured cloths and napkins and match both the flowers and the food with them. You may get an all pink or an all white meal or lovely, multi-coloured food and flowers against a gold cloth.

We British are more conventional and most people today have polished tables with table mats to protect the polish from hot plates. Have a best set of mats for parties; you can actually make these quite easily yourself from old prints. I also like lace over round, gold-painted cork mats.

Paper napkins should only be used at children's parties and if you find linen napkins expensive to buy, make your own, which you will find very inexpensive.

Cutlery on a dinner table is placed so that the guest takes the outside things first, working inwards. For a typical meal the cutlery on the right-hand side will be (right to left) soup spoon, fish, meat and bread-and-butter knives; on the left-hand side (left to right) fish fork and meat fork. Above the place mat are the pudding spoon and fork set in opposite directions with the handles to the right and left respectively.

The glasses are just to the right. On the left

142

is a bread plate.

Because I like amusing, stimulating conversation at my parties, I have a refectory table which is narrow enough for my guests to be able to talk to the person opposite them as well as to those on either side.

The only disadvantage is that if we are eight and my husband sits at the head of the table, I cannot sit at the opposite end. To place men and women alternately, a hostess must sit on the side, while a man occupies her usual chair at the foot of the table.

The Queen and Prince Philip at their private luncheon parties sit on either side of the table facing each other. It keeps conversation flowing and gives an air of informality.

When the guests arrive to dine with me, the door is opened by my butler or parlourmaid who takes the man's coat and hat and says to the lady:

'Would you like to put your wrap upstairs, Madam?'

Without staff: Your husband opens the door, shakes hands with the guests and suggests that the men put their coats and hats down in the hall. He says to the women: 'Would you like to go upstairs? You will find my wife's bedroom if you turn left on the top landing.'

* * * *

Some women, if they have only come a short

distance, leave their cloaks in the hall, but others go upstairs. They are met by a housemaid and shown into a bedroom. Here the lights are on and there are combs, and powder on the dressing table and clean towels in the adjoining bathroom.

Without staff: Do be careful to leave your bedroom tidy and your bathroom neat and pretty. I hate using bathrooms where people leave stockings dripping on the rail, old hot water bottles on the door and rather nasty looking toothbrushes above the basin. If you have a spare room it is a good idea to send your guests in there rather than use your own bedroom. But do remember they will require combs, powder, clean towels etc.

★ ★ ★ ★

The male guest waits in the hall until his wife, or the lady he is escorting, returns. Then the butler leads the way to the drawing-room and, going in first, announces, 'Mr and Mrs Bofkins'.

I come forward, shake hands first with the wife and then with the husband. My husband follows and does the same.

Without staff: Your husband waits until the guests are assembled and then says: 'Come into the sitting room', and brings them in to you. You exclaim: 'How lovely to see you!' or something really welcoming as you shake hands.

★ ★ ★ ★

I take Mrs. Bofkins up to the most important lady present whom we will call Mrs Snooks.

I say: 'Mrs Snooks, may I introduce Mrs Bofkins?' After they have shaken hands, I introduce Mrs Bofkins to the other women present and then to the men, saying, in this case, to her:

'May I introduce Colonel Thompson?' or, as an alternative: 'Do you know Colonel Thompson?'

It is usual for the husband to follow behind his wife shaking hands—which makes a double introduction unnecessary. If he is held up by my husband talking to him, then I take him round as soon as his wife knows everybody.

My husband asks them what they will drink and fetches the cocktails, sherry or tomato juice. When everybody has arrived he usually takes the cocktail shaker round again, filling up the glasses.

Without staff: You do exactly the same, making sure not only that everybody is introduced but, if they are strangers to one another, starting a topic of conversation before you turn away to greet other guests. If your husband is opening the door to newcomers you will have to pour the drinks or ask one of the first male arrivals to help you.

★ ★ ★ ★

You must never force your guests to drink. The person who invariably forces drinks on everyone he meets is often suffering from an inferiority complex.

When dinner is ready, the butler comes into the room and says to me in quite a low voice: 'Dinner is served, Madam.'

Without staff: When everyone has arrived you slip away unobtrusively. In the kitchen the daily help will be waiting to serve up what you have already cooked earlier in the day. You tell her you are ready to start. Then return to the sitting-room.

★ ★ ★ ★

When I hear that dinner is ready I turn to the most important lady present, and say: 'Mrs Snooks, will you come in to dinner?' The women then all move towards the door, followed by the men. I usually go beside Mrs Snooks, both to show her the way and help people find their places.

When we are ten I put the names on small cards and place them just above the table mats. But whether I have name-cards or not, I always have a rough plan in my hand so that I can direct people to their seats.

Mrs Snooks, of course, sits on my husband's right, the next most important lady on his left. Mr Snooks is on my right. But with a lot of married couples as guests it is not always possible in a small party to put everyone in their correct precedence and keep husbands and wives apart.

For a dinner party of eight or ten I have four courses:

> Fish or soup
> Meat or game
> An exciting pudding
> Savoury
> Dessert
> Coffee

Without staff: Three courses will be plenty for your party. If you are wise you will start with a cold dish. Prawn cocktail, melon, eggs in aspic or hors-d'œuvre are all easy to serve. The first three can already be on the table in front of the guests. The hors d'œuvre, on a big dish, is passed round by your husband.

'... MAY I INTRODUCE?'

Soup is usually the only dish served by the butler. The tureen stands on a side-table and he ladles the soup into each plate before it is served to the guest.

The wines we give our guests for a big party are: white wine, champagne with the pudding, port with the dessert, liqueurs after the coffee. This means that beside each guest's place are a wine glass, a champagne glass and a tumbler in case they prefer water.

When there are servants, the plates for the first course are never put on the table until everyone is seated. Napkins, folded elegantly, are in front of everyone's place. Napkin rings are never used at the dinner table.

The food is served to the lady on my husband's right and the servant then proceeds straight round the table. In foreign countries the ladies are all served before the gentlemen, who watch the intricate weaving in and out with hungry eyes.

Meat and game are usually carved in the kitchen, and put on a dish decorated with vegetables. Guests always help themselves. Only a salad can be served individually, on an extra kidney-shaped glass dish which is placed on the left of the plate.

If a guest refuses a dish, the plate is removed immediately, also the knife and fork or whatever implement would have been used for that course.

148

Without staff: Have as a main course something which can be kept hot in the oven, like creamed chicken, an Italian pilaf or a roast leg of lamb. If you have the last, get your husband to carve it before the guests arrive and then rearrange the meat into its original uncarved shape. Then your help can place the vegetables around the dish at the last moment. In this way there will only be gravy to be handed as an extra. As your third course have another cold dish. Lemon soufflé served with sliced oranges is delicious. If you prefer a savoury, stuffed eggs or celery filled with cream cheese is excellent.

SOUP IS SERVED BY THE BUTLER

When the savoury is finished the table is cleared of everything except the salt cellars if the dessert includes nuts. Bread and toast crumbs are brushed from the table with a folded napkin on to a silver salver or a plate.

The finger bowls are then put in front of each guest. These bowls are already on the plates with a small lace mat underneath them and a silver dessert fork and knife on either side of them. The bowls are half filled with water and it is a pretty idea to have a small flower head floating in each one.

Without staff: You and your husband clear away the plates and put the dessert plates in front of your guests and the bowls of dessert on the table so that they can help themselves.

★ ★ ★ ★

The guest lifts the finger bowl and lace mat on to the table. Dessert is offered in the same way as the other courses, but the dishes are then set down in the middle of the table. The port glasses are now put beside each guest— they are never included with the other glasses.

Port starts with the guest on the host's right and goes round the table clockwise. The decanter must never be reversed. There is a great deal of superstition about this and most people believe it to be unlucky. I even heard someone say it originated at the Last Supper.

The rule that port should go round the table

YOU AND YOUR HUSBAND CLEAR AWAY
THE PLATES

151

started late in the Georgian era. Until then port had never been kept but was drunk as soon as it was bottled, and was, in consequence, quite weak and rather like Vin Rosé. Then someone started to 'put it down' and vintage port came into fashion.

At a dinner party a bottle of vintage port would be produced and the first gentleman would help himself, finish his glass while his neighbour was filling his and take the bottle back for another helping. This meant the gentlemen further down the table were often unable to sample it. So the rule was made that the port could not reverse.

Without staff: Your husband puts the port glasses beside each guest, offers port to the lady on his right then sits down and passes the decanter to the guests on his left.

*   *   *   *

Coffee is served in small cups, and the guests usually help themselves to sugar, cream and coffee.

Coffee must never be served in the cup. Tea is never offered at English dinners, but Americans and Canadians in their own countries usually drink tea or coffee all through the meal in breakfast-sized cups.

When the ladies have finished their port or liqueurs, I glance at Mrs Snooks and we rise simultaneously from the table, followed by the other ladies. The gentlemen stand and the one nearest the door opens it.

When the ladies have left the dining-room, the men move up the table to sit near my husband and the port is then passed round again. The brandy and other liqueurs are also in front of him.

Outside in the hall I ask the ladies if they would like to go upstairs; if anyone says 'Yes', I take her upstairs while the others go into the drawing-room.

We are joined there by the gentlemen in about fifteen minutes.

Without staff: Your help hands the coffee on a tray through the dining-room door—or you fetch it from the kitchen—and sets it down in front of you. You serve each guest, asking them if they like milk and sugar.

When you leave the dining-room you ask your chief guest, or someone you know well, to take the ladies upstairs. You then hurry into the sitting-room and remove the used cocktail glasses and tidy the room. You then go and join the ladies.

★ ★ ★ ★

I prefer conversation at my parties, but my daughter and her husband frequently have Bridge parties. In this case the host and hostess play at separate tables.

At about 10.30 it is usual for the host to offer the men a whisky and soda or a glass of beer—

the ladies often have a soft drink. When these are finished, it is a signal for the guests to take their leave.

The whole secret of giving a good dinner party lies in mixing people who will like and amuse each other.

Without staff: The secret of making your party a success is not to appear flustered or worried. Be sure to have food you can cook well and easily. If you have no help at all arrange with your husband to alternate with you in collecting things from the kitchen so that your guests are never left alone.

If your daily help has to be taken home after the party—which is usual in country districts—your husband must slip away quietly when the gentlemen leave the dining-room.

If you have no help you do the washing up after the guests have gone or the next morning. You never embarrass your guests by doing it while they are there and so putting them in the position of having to offer to help you.

* * * *

Dressing for dinner

I must make some mention of dressing for dinner. In Great Britain we have always made dinner a somewhat ceremonial meal. At the beginning of the century it would have been unthinkable for any folk who called themselves lady or gentleman to sit down to dinner except in evening dress. We all know the jokes about Englishmen who change into their tail coats in the middle of the jungle.

Cocktail parties have spoilt this because they go on so late; but I think it is dirty and slovenly for people to have dinner in the clothes they have worn all day, though I am not suggesting for a moment that women who cook their own meals and husbands who help with the washing up should put on elaborate evening clothes.

If you want to enjoy a good meal do wash and change. A bath before dinner is, to my mind, a necessity; but a good wash is essential. Then put on something attractive, but comfortable, and enjoy yourself.

I am really shocked by many people who, having been born into a position to know better, even when they have servants, rush in to dinner unwashed and with dirty shoes— the men often without a tie.

When friends who are inviting you out say 'don't change', what they mean is 'don't wear evening dress'. For a man this means a plain navy or dark grey suit but for a woman a cocktail dress—i.e. an afternoon dress with a lowish neck in silk, lace or some light material. *Note*. It is wise to take a fur stole or a scarf when dining in country houses.

Buffet dinners

I hate holding a plate and fork in one hand, a glass in the other and trying to eat. But buffet dinners are an excellent way of entertaining a lot of people. In India buffet dinners are beautifully done and the food is nearly always arranged on a refectory table in the centre of the room.

At all buffet meals guests help themselves from a variety of dishes, but I always try to make these easy to eat with a fork. Mousses, small vol-au-vents, cream of salmon and sausages on sticks are all excellent.

The only necessity for servants at a buffet dinner is for them to collect the dirty plates and open the bottles of wine.

BUFFET DINNERS

Luncheon parties

Luncheon parties follow exactly the same etiquette as a dinner party. The courses are offered as at a dinner party. A luncheon menu is usually:

Omelette or prawn cocktail
Meat, chicken or game
Apple meringue or some such pudding
Cheese and biscuits
Coffee

The wine is light—vin rosé is very popular at the moment. Port is sometimes offered at more formal luncheons.

The table is not cleared with the cheese course as at dinner, and finger bowls are not used because you never have dessert at lunch.

Cocktail parties

If these are large you will need servants to take round the trays of drink; but with any number under thirty it is quite easy for the host or hostess to manage them on their own.

Do not make the cocktails too strong and make a popular one like gin and orange, or a dry martini. As an alternative have sherry and tomato juice. If you can afford it most men prefer whisky and soda.

Plates of delicious things should be put on occasional tables for people to help themselves.

COCKTAIL PARTIES

Male guests can also be asked to help pass them around.

Supper parties

After cocktail parties or because they can't afford anything elaborate, people say 'Come to supper.' This can be a very simple meal of one main dish with fruit or cheese to follow and a bottle of Vin Rosé or Chianti.

Any of the Italian dishes of pasta are excellent for this and I would rather have a really ripe Camembert or Brie than anything a chef can produce.

Be careful that your cheeses are ripe and put your biscuits in the oven, then serve them hot, neatly arranged in rows on a tray. They both look and taste nicer that way.

The whole success of a supper party of this kind is to have plenty of the main course for hungry men and, of course, it must be really well cooked.

If your guests are likely to be late or unpunctual, have hot soup and everything else cold. Or prepare the meal up to the last minute then finish it off in the dining-room in an electric chafing dish.

Toasts

When drinking a cocktail or any other drink it is completely wrong to say: 'Cheers!', 'Here's how!', 'Mud in your eye', 'Happy

Days!' or any other toast. At the same time if someone makes a toast it would be bad manners not to respond.

Times for parties

Coffee mornings	11.0 a.m.
Luncheon	1.0 or 1.30 p.m.
Tea Parties	4.0 or 4.30 p.m.
Dinner	Between 7.30 and 9 p.m.
Dances	Between 10 and 11 p.m.
Supper (formal)	10.30 or 11 p.m.
Supper (informal and instead of Dinner)	9 p.m. onwards
Fêtes, Bazaars etc.	2.30 p.m.
Garden Parties	3.0 to 6.30 p.m. or 4.0 to 7.30 p.m.
Cocktails	6.0 or 6.30 p.m. to 7.30 or 8 p.m.

VARIOUS SORTS OF PARTIES

The cocktail-cum-dinner party

Guests are asked at 6.30 or 7 p.m. in the usual way. Cocktails are served until about 8.30 or 9 p.m. when there is a Buffet supper. Dancing to small band or radiogram. No one wears evening dress.

Dinner dances

This can be very much the same as the cocktail party but guests are asked later and it can be much more elaborate. Some hostesses prefer to give a big dinner dance for their debutante daughter rather than to have the trouble of arranging a number of separate dinner parties.

The dinner dances I give in the country are proper sit-down dinner parties at eight o'clock for eight or sixteen young people. Afterwards I have a pianist and they dance until 12.30 a.m. Most people, of course, will prefer to use a record player.

I do not provide an elaborate buffet as the young people have had a four-course dinner. At about 10.45 p.m. my guests are offered hot sausages on cocktail sticks, pâté sandwiches, vol-au-vents and ice cream. Soft drinks, beer, cider, wine or fruit cup are on a side table in the room where they dance.

Informal parties

More and more people give parties as part of the Christmas seasonal festivities, at the New Year, in order to enhance friendship in the neighbourhood, to introduce a new neighbour to the other families in the district, or 'for no reason at all except that we like parties'—which is probably the best motive of any.

The usual starting time is 7.30—8 p.m. and because the party is informal verbal invitations are better than written ones. Extend your invitations ten days to a fortnight ahead so that people can make arrangements and you can manipulate the numbers according to the number of acceptances. Try to send all the invitations on the same day so that no one gets the impression that theirs is an afterthought.

The way to ensure success is to invite people of whom fifty per cent know one another and fifty per cent are strangers. Relatives, the husband's business friends, and neighbours are obvious examples of hitherto unacquainted groups.

The hostess who goes in for too elaborate a show will not only exhaust herself but embarrass some guests who cast their minds back to their own more modest efforts and ponder on the need to change their plans for a future simple party in their homes.

A reasonably simple affair which runs smoothly will be infinitely more enjoyable than an ostentatious party full of risks that things may go wrong.

A buffet party for twelve to fifteen people can be agreeably organised by a hostess with little or no help. The food, which should be plentiful, can be quite simple, and restricted to items which can be eaten with a fork or the fingers. Drinks need not be elaborate— a punch is an economical idea if well made and a reliable recipe meticulously followed.

One important thing is to have far more plates, cutlery and glasses than you imagine can possibly be used. They will be—and it will save a lot of annoyance. Plates are cheap to hire (don't economise on washing up by using paper picnic plates), and most off-licence firms today have arrangements to hire glasses.

A buffet party at which the food is appetising and the drinks well planned will need no further organisation. It is not advisable to plan a schedule of games—which half the people will not like— and it is certainly bad taste to arrange an event at which the guests will be passive participants, such as screening one's holiday transparencies, running off some allegedly amusing rigmarole on a tape recorder or—most heinous sin of all—insisting on watching some TV programme.

Guests will be expected to leave some time after 11 p.m. If it is winter time a final drink from bottles kept in reserve, or better still if some of the guests are motoring, an offer of coffee, will be acceptable.

This not only gives a finishing touch to the party but helps to bridge that awkward gap when guests are uncertain whether they should leave and the host does not want to be too pointed about the lateness of the hour.

The buffet party, on simpler lines as regards the amount of food and drink, is a pleasant method of entertaining after a group of friends have visited a theatre or concert. Everything can, of course, be prepared beforehand. It is not usual for such an occasion to last for more than an hour.

Teen-agers' parties

Teen-age sons and daughters love to have a few friends around, and the buffet type of party is ideal. Although the younger generation have strong ideas on what not to have at these affairs they are very vague on what they really want. On the amusement side they can be left to themselves—and should be—but the food and drink are their elders' responsibility.

Even though they may like to appear grown up they have children's appetites, and the great secret is to provide plenty of food. The Swiss cheese fondue dish is not only delicious and filling, but good fun as the guests all dip in the bowl. Drinks should be soft—or at the most a very innocuous fruit punch—and there should be plenty of that teen-age standby: coffee.

Barbecue parties

This is, of course, the modern teen-ager's idea of convivial paradise, and more and more adults insist that they enjoy them too.

Unfortunately, the barbecue party in my experience is rarely successful, because the weather cannot be relied upon. Moving the barbecue to an empty garage in order to get the charcoal burning and to keep the guests out of the wind and the rain is not the average person's idea of a happy evening. As for the host who has planned everything so carefully, and spent so much on expensive steaks, the climatic ruination of all the careful preparations is unjustly disheartening.

In Britain, at any rate, it is wiser to make all evening parties indoor affairs. If the cult of the steak is so inexorably attractive, a grill in the kitchen can do all that the barbecue does—and a lot more appetisingly.

... KEEP THE GUESTS OUT OF THE WIND AND RAIN

165

Wine and cheese parties

An inexpensive and informal party is a wine and cheese party. This can be held either at 6.30—8 p.m. or after 9 p.m.— the implication being that it is not a substitute for dinner.

You can create a theme for the party by having nothing but English cheeses, or nothing but French or Swiss ones; or a galaxy of them all, which could mean thirty or forty even of the best-known kinds. However simple or elaborate your range of cheeses, get the genuine kind—not the processed horrors. Each cheese should be on a separate dish or plate so that the guests can cut the amount they want.

Several kinds of biscuits, and of bread, should be provided, and lots of butter.

As regards the wines there is no need for anything expensive. It is usual to serve white wines, which on the whole are cheaper, quality for quality, than red ones. At least three or four kinds should be provided—say French, Italian, German and Spanish. Supplying wine on the basis of each guest drinking one-third of a bottle should be plenty even if the party is so successful that the guests stay longer than expected.

What wine and when?

Many people do not order wine with a meal because they are afraid of making a social mistake in the kind they choose.

Most of the pompous advice given by the newspapers and magazines by self-appointed experts is—just jargon. It is a form of snobbishness eagerly cultivated by the vintners who find it profitable to encourage the view that a certain vintage or year is very special and can therefore be sold at inflated prices.

Of course after a lifetime of wine-drinking your palate may, perhaps, become discriminating enough to relish the niceties of bouquet; but you may rightly be suspicious of the man who pretends to know all there is to know about wine.

'It's a naive domestic Burgundy without any breeding but I think you'll be amused by its presumption', was the caption to a Thurber drawing of a wine snob intimidating his guests.

You can enhance your social prestige and your reputation as a good host or hostess by offering wine to your guests. You will please your host if you show an intelligent interest and genuine taste for the wine he gives you.

Wines at dinner

The correct times for wines at a dinner party are as follows:

1. Serve sherry with the soup, but if people have had cocktails or sherry before dinner, this is unnecessary. If you start the dinner with clear soup, it is a good idea to add a little sherry in the kitchen before it comes

into the dining room.
2. White wine with the fish course.
3. Red wine with the meat.
4. Champagne with the pudding.
5. Port with the dessert.
6. Liqueurs after the coffee.

Now *all* these wines are served only at a Banquet or a very grand dinner party. Most people have white wine with the fish and red wine with the meat, and perhaps port or brandy afterwards.

Others offer their guests a choice of red or white wine.

These two rules are important:

1. The white wine should be cooled. Put it in the refrigerator or in a bucket of cold water about tea time and it will be perfect.
2. Claret should be decanted. Burgundy can be served in the bottle. Both should be left in a warm atmosphere for several hours before dinner.

How to serve white wine

White wine is left in the bottle and served as it is. A tip to those who are not wealthy is that any quite cheap white wine, if sufficiently chilled, tastes good.

Champagne

Champagne is wrapped in a table napkin

before it is served. Put it in the refrigerator for two hours before the guests arrive.

Port

Port is always decanted. Liqueurs are served as they are bought.

Decanters

Decanters—old cut glass ones—can be bought for about 10/- at almost any antique shop. Keep one for sherry, one for port. Old silver or enamel labels look nice and prevent you mixing them up. The Claret decanter should, to be correct, have a handle. I bought a delightful one last year with a silver neck for 15/-.

Glasses

Don't be afraid of making wine an integral part of your entertaining because of the expense of different glasses and the worry of knowing which to use. If you want to be meticulously correct you can buy these glasses:

> For sherry; a thin elongated glass rather like an inverted dunce's cap on a short stem.
> For red and white table wine; a largish tulip-shaped glass on a medium length stem.
> For hock; a tulip-shaped cup, usually tinted, on a very long stem.

For port; the same height as the sherry glass but with a round bowl.

For champagne; a wide, shallow cup on a medium stem.

For liqueurs; a small thimble-sized glass.

For brandy; a balloon shaped glass.

Charming as this glassware is, you will offend no one if you use just one shape—a tulip of medium size on a medium stem. In France—in most restaurants, apart from those who inflate bills—all wines will be served in this kind of glass.

It is wise to have the special glasses described above for liqueurs. This is not so much a social convention as a means of economy. This type of glass was a trade invention to make the drink look more than, in fact, it was.

The secret of having any successful party lies in introducing your guests properly.

Introduction

English people are hopeless at introductions and therefore never remember names. Americans have a maddening habit of repeating your name over and over again, but it does fix it in their minds.

'How do you do, Miss Cartland,' they say. 'How are you, Miss Cartland? Now do tell me, Miss Cartland, when were you last in the U.S.A.?'

By this time you are sick of the sound of your name, but they never forget it.

One vital point is to say the names of those you introduce clearly and never for one moment stop introducing.

A good hostess has no time at her own party for prolonged conversation. Her job is to see that other people enjoy themselves and have the opportunity to meet many more friends.

Choosing the guests

Remember, too, when you are choosing your guests, that it is a fatal mistake to have nothing but stars. The more distinguished the guest, the larger the audience needed.

I once went to a dinner party where there were three Dukes, two Ambassadors and two distinguished visitors from overseas. It was a flop! No one wanted to listen to anyone else and there were no admiring fans.

A celebrity or two amongst a group of people ready to be impressed guarantees the success of a party. But avoid having more than two or three 'social lions' at the same time. They think they are in the right place because the other is there, and are not eclipsed by too much competition.

Entertaining in a restaurant

With the shortage of servants a great many people entertain in restaurants, especially when business is involved. The host should book a table, and for any party over six it is wise to choose both the dinner and the wines beforehand. This dispenses with endless discussion and any possible embarrassment by guests who do not wish to ask for anything too expensive.

... TWO OR THREE SOCIAL LIONS

172

A gentleman tells the head waiter who he is, then lets his lady guests walk first behind the waiter who leads them to their table. It is a sign of bad breeding for a man to walk in either first, or smoking, or with both hands in his trouser pockets.

The wine waiter will show the wine which has been ordered to the host before he opens it, to make sure it is correct. The host usually just nods his head.

The waiter will then pour a little wine into the host's glass. He will taste it and again nod his head unless there is something very obviously wrong with it.

You may, if you really know wine, complain about the temperature if it is wrong by your reliable experience; about the taste if you consider it is different from what that vintage and name imply; about the wine being corked if it really is. But do be careful.

I heard a man make a terrible gaffe in a restaurant by saying loudly: 'This wine is corked' and then showing a small piece of cork floating in his glass!

Pieces of cork falling into the wine from the hole made by the corkscrew do not make a wine 'corked'. A good waiter will not let this happen, but if it does, it will not affect the taste of the wine.

Corking is the contamination of the wine by a cork which has dried out and dropped a deposit of dust in the wine, or otherwise contaminated the liquor. The taste is unforgettable and nauseating. There can be no doubt that the wine is bad when this happens and no waiter will ever query the matter or refuse to change the bottle.

In France you always tip the wine waiter after a meal regardless of the fact that there is a service charge on the bill. In England if you have a large party and a lot of wines in smart restaurants it is usual to give the wine waiter 10/- or £1; but there is no real necessity to do this if you have already given 15 per cent on the bill.

Waiters are tipped on the plate when the bill is paid and not individually. In the country one gives 10 per cent of the bill, i.e. 2/- in the pound; in London $12\frac{1}{2}$ to 15 per cent, i.e. 2/6d. to 3/-.

If one is known to the restaurant it is much better manners to ask the management to allow you to sign the bill, or even to send it to you the following day.

It is usual to offer one's guests cocktails in the lounge first and also to have the coffee served there when the dinner is finished.

In London restaurants a man arriving for lunch or dinner should take his hat and coat straight to the cloakroom. Then he goes into the lounge to look for his friends. The same applies to a woman at dinner time if she is wearing a coat. Most women keep on a fur stole during the winter. Both men and women always tip in the cloakroom. 1/- is the average tip.

If the party go on to a theatre or a night club after dinner, the host tips the doorman for fetching a taxi or opening the door of his car. He also offers to pay for a taxi if they have all ridden in it. But usually the male guests will insist on sharing this.

It is quite usual, if the host has paid for dinner and perhaps a theatre, for the male guests to offer a contribution towards the expenses of a night club. But a host must not expect this and will only accept if he knows the guests are able to afford it.

It is inexcusable for a host to take his party on to a night club and then go home without offering to pay for *everything*. It is his evening out and he is responsible for every expense.

If there are single women in the party the host must make sure that a man sees them home; failing this, he must do so himself.

Guests to stay

With the shortage of servants and money entertaining has grown not only much less, but much more slipshod. Hosts ask people to 'come and find us as we are', which usually means that they aren't going to take much trouble. Also I find few people make their guests

175

really comfortable, mostly because they live uncomfortably themselves.

I think, if you do have friends to stay, they should be properly looked after. Here is the correct way to do this; and if you have no staff, you can do a great deal yourself unostentatiously.

Male guests to stay

The formal routine when a guest arrives at an important house is as follows:

His luggage is carried upstairs and unpacked. If he arrives at 6 o'clock his dinner jacket is put

GUESTS TO STAY

ready on the chair for him to change into. His evening shoes, socks, underclothes and shirt with the studs all ready in the cuffs are also put out. A bath is drawn ready in the bathroom and a towel put over the chair.

Without staff: If you have no help, your husband should offer to carry your guest's cases upstairs. Make sure the guest knows where his bath towel is and see that there is a new cake of soap for him to use, fresh towels and a clean bath mat.

Shoes to be cleaned

After the guest has gone down to dinner, the clothes he has been wearing are taken away and pressed and his shoes cleaned.

Without staff: You obviously don't press your guest's clothes but you must look into his room when he has gone down to dinner. Put his clothes tidily over the chair if he hasn't already done so or hang them in the wardrobe. Take his shoes away to be cleaned and turn down the bed clothes.

★　★　★　★

I am giving the correct etiquette from a host's point of view, but I realise that this could be embarrassing for some guests, and as the object of good manners is to give no hurt and cause no offence it is clearly the duty of a host to disregard custom should he suspect that the guest is unaware of correct procedure.

Thus some people, not too well off, a little shy, or unaccustomed to visiting other people's homes, might well be worried or even annoyed should their clothes be unpacked when they arrive or tidied after they have changed for the evening.

One must cultivate the sensitivity to know a guest's probable reactions. But there can be no possible objection to showing care and attention to the guest's comfort by turning down the bed, drawing the curtains, and so on.

Orders for breakfast

After dinner in the big household where the full complement of staff is employed the butler goes into the drawing-room and says: 'What orders for the morning, Madam?' The hostess asks the guest what time he would like to be called with his breakfast and whether he prefers tea or coffee.

Without staff: You ask your guest what time he wants his breakfast and if you do the work of the house yourself you will doubtless find it far easier for him to have his breakfast in bed. It is an awful bother when you are clearing the sitting-room to have someone sitting about and considerate guests will keep out of the way until latish in the morning unless something specific has been arranged for them.

* * * *

Female guests to stay

In the household with staff the housemaid unpacks, asks what dress the guest is going to wear that night and presses it if necessary. A bath is prepared; and a quarter of an hour before dinner the housemaid knocks at the bedroom door and enquires if the lady wishes her dress to be done up.

Without staff: You offer to help your guest unpack. Be sure she has lots of coat-hangers in her bedroom and empty drawers. (Clean paper should have been put in these before she arrives.)

BREAKFAST IN BED

Hot water bottles

The housemaid also asks if the guest needs a hot-water bottle (good guests bring their own) and what are the orders for the morning?

Everything the guest wears, including her underclothes and nightgown, is pressed after she has worn them.

Without staff: Always have a spare hot-water bottle in the house or you will find guests borrowing yours while you lie shivering in bed. Put an electric kettle in the guest room so they can fill their own bottles with really hot water.

* * * *

Arrangements for the night

The guest's nightgown and dressing gown are laid out on a chair, her slippers on the floor in front of them. The bed is turned down, the curtains and blinds drawn.

Newspapers

These are a most important comfort and nothing is more annoying than for a guest to find, when he or she comes downstairs, that everyone is talking about a crisis reported in the newspapers and to know nothing about it.

Early morning tea

At the beginning of the century all guests had early morning tea when they were called, but with staff difficulties it has gone out of fashion.

It is usual to ask guests if they want it, unless they have breakfast in bed. Then they are called and their breakfast brought in on a tray immediately afterwards.

Breakfasts

If the guests breakfast upstairs, the hostess asks if they want a 'cooked or uncooked breakfast'.

'Cooked' means eggs and bacon or fish, which should be sent up on a plate with a cover to keep it warm. Besides this the tray will contain all the ingredients of an 'uncooked' breakfast. These are, tea or coffee (both in pots, of course), milk, sugar, a rack of toast, butter, marmalade or honey, fruit—either an apple or a small bunch of grapes.

Without staff: Tell your woman guest frankly what time you want her to appear in the morning. If you are doing everything yourself a considerate friend will not expect a cooked breakfast. Tea, toast and marmalade is quite enough but add some fruit to the tray if you can.

★ ★ ★ ★

If the guests come downstairs to breakfast, they eat the same as the host and hostess. Cereals or porridge is provided in most houses before the eggs and bacon, and if there is a large party it is usual to have a cold ham on the sideboard. Even when there are servants in the house guests wait on themselves at breakfast.

181

Extra comforts in the bedroom

Water in a jug with a top, and a glass;
Biscuits in an airtight tin;
A reading lamp beside the bed.
A clock which works;
An electric or gas fire;
An electric kettle so that guests can fill their
    own hot-water bottle;
Writing paper, envelopes and ink;
A card stating the time the post leaves;
Books—a selection for all tastes;
Plenty of coat-hangers;
Lights on the dressing table so that the wom-
    en can see to make-up;
Most important—a comfortable bed and an
    extra blanket.

I have suffered so badly from hard beds in
other people's houses that I now have a special
feather overlay which packs into a small zip
bag. It may be doubtful manners to take it
with me, but hosts who sleep on 'powder
puffs' themselves give their guests mattresses
which haven't had anything done to them for
half a century.

All mattresses should be made over every
five years. It is not very expensive and it is
abominable bad manners to make your guests
suffer a sleepless night because you are too lazy
or too mean to give them a decent bed.

I like blinds in a bedroom because the light

wakes me. A comfortable bedroom should always have them or interlined curtains.

In the bathroom

A large bath towel and a face towel for each guest. If more than one person is using the bathroom an extra bath-mat is a good idea and two tooth glasses. Other comforts include:

Bath powder;
Bath oil or salts for softening and scenting the water;
Soft lavatory paper.

Good-byes

On all occasions in a private house guests should be seen off on the doorstep by the host or a member of his family. The host waits at the door until the guests have driven off in their cars, and waves as they move away.

Seven

THE IDEAL GUEST

Punctuality

The golden rule for a guest is punctuality. There is a silly idea among some young people that it is smart to arrive late. If an invitation says 'Dinner 8.00' it means that the guests should arrive at a few minutes to eight.

It involves some trouble to gauge one's time of arrival to a nicety and as I am over-punctual my husband and I often have to drive around the neighbourhood until we can arrive on the doorstep at exactly the right moment. In private houses a guest should always be downstairs five minutes before a meal.

On being introduced

When being introduced, the usual thing is to shake hands and say 'How do you do?' and neither to expect or give an answer. It is not correct to say 'Pleased to meet you.' A handshake should be waist high and neither limp nor overpowering. It is important to smile pleasantly at each person to whom you are introduced, looking them straight in the eyes.

It is good manners when being introduced to just one person, or in the case of a group when introduced to the last one, for a guest to

184

start a conversation and keep it going. There is nothing more awkward than an awful silence between two people who have just been made known to one another because neither can think of anything to say.

A guest must get it firmly into his head that he is expected to pay for his dinner by being charming and entertaining. It is essential for children to learn to make conversation whenever they have meals with friends of their parents or friends of their own.

'Talk!', I used to say to my daughter. 'It doesn't matter what you say, but it's abominably rude to sit eating and saying nothing.'

She protested that at parties she would catch my eye, know I was expecting her to speak and everything would fly out of her head. But anyone sitting next to Lady Lewisham today would be very surprised if she was not entertaining and stimulating.

Smoking at dinner

Hostesses are, in these days, resigned to the fact that many guests, especially Americans, light a cigarette between courses. I always enjoy a story of the Earl of Caernarvon who has an excellent chef and takes a great deal of trouble over his food.

An American guest took out her cigarette case after the fish course had been served and said:

'You don't mind if I smoke?'

'Of course not,' Lord Caernarvon answered and, turning to his butler, said: 'Bring the coffee!"

The American realised what she had done and cried, 'Oh, I'm so sorry. If you mind, of course I won't smoke!'

'But I don't mind,' Lord Caernarvon answered. 'If you have finished your dinner you will, of course, want to smoke and I will cancel the other courses.'

The guest apologised and dinner was resumed, but I'm sure she never offended again.

I think smoking during a meal is an insult to the cook and one's hostess; but I am too polite to say so at the time. I just don't invite the person again.

Conversation

During the meal and afterwards, no guest, however delightful he or she may find their partner on the right or left, should talk only to that particular person. The conversation swings automatically from side to side and the moment a guest sees that the person on one side of him has no one to talk to, he must turn and start a new conversation.

During the evening men must restrain themselves from indulging too long in chats on exclusively masculine topics, while it is very wrong for a woman to chatter with other

women across the table unless it is on a subject
likely to interest their male partners.

Guests

Guests are expected to eat what is put in front
of them and look as though they are enjoying
it. But second helpings are not usually offered
at dinner—although a very delicious pudding
is sometimes made the exception.

Refusing food

If someone is on a strict diet, it is better not to
go out to meals. Nothing is more maddening
for a hostess than to plan a delicious lunch or

SMOKING AT DINNER

187

dinner and offer it to a guest who says plaintively that she can only eat raw carrots or a lettuce leaf! If you are dieting help yourself to a very tiny helping and play about with it until the other people finish.

If you do have to refuse food because it always disagrees with you, there is no reason to go into the details for not eating it. There is nothing more boring than to have someone describe eagerly how she is allergic to duck or to listen to a long monologue about what happened when someone ate a bad oyster.

Table manners

> 'I eat my peas with honey;
> I've done so all my life.
> It makes the peas taste funny,
> But they stick upon my knife.'

Despite all the allegations about ill-bred people who eat peas with a knife or splutter in their soup, the average person will never meet anyone who does this sort of thing.

However, we are all at some time young enough, and most of us at some time inexperienced enough, to meet situations which are new, either because of the company, the food, or possibly the country.

There need be no difficulty over which knife and fork to use in this country because you take the outside ones and work towards the centre.

In other countries, and in the homes of foreigners, there may be a problem, particularly if the economical custom of using the same knife and fork for another course is followed. If so, there will be cutlery rests provided. The only solution when in doubt is to imitate your host.

When to use a spoon

In Britain a soup spoon is round and the soup is drunk from the side nearest you. You fill your spoon sideways from the other side of the dish; and in order to do this you may tilt your soup plate away from you—not towards you—if necessary. In Europe the soup spoons are invariably pointed at the tip because the soup is drunk with the tip put in the mouth.

With other courses it is not correct to use a dessert spoon alone. A fork alone is all right for any dish but a dessert spoon must be accompanied by a fork. A teaspoon for an ice is correct.

Fish forks

Fish knives were not invented until Victoria came to the throne. There is nothing wrong in using them; it is merely that they are a comparative innovation and people who are proud of their antique Georgian silver look on them with scorn.

Oysters

Oysters are eaten with a special fork—or an ordinary fork—and must be swallowed, not chewed. A gourmet will insist that the liquor in the shell has a bouquet which must not be missed and he will pick it up and tip the liquor into his mouth.

Hors d'œuvres

Hors d'œuvres are always eaten with a fork unless ham or large pieces of sausage are included.

Bread

In France and almost everywhere else in Europe it is quite correct to use a piece of bread in the left hand as an aid to eating—but not in England. Bread or toast is always broken by hand at luncheon or dinner and never cut with a knife.

Asparagus

Asparagus (except the very thin tips from the garden) is picked up in the right hand. Dipped in melted butter or in hollandaise sauce, one eats the tip and as much of the stalk as is edible. Finger bowls are always put on the table after the asparagus has been served, and are taken away when finished.

Meat or game

For meat or game a knife and fork are used the whole time. The American custom of cutting everything up and then eating with the fork only is, to us, very clumsy. The first finger of each hand points half-way down the implement. It is wrong to hold either knife or fork as one holds a pencil. The hand goes over the handle.

Dessert

Fresh fruit like apples and pears should be eaten with a silver knife and fork. Fruit should be cut in halves or quarters with the fruit knife, and these sections peeled. The edible portions are then conveyed to the mouth with the fork, first being cut small enough for this.

Soft fresh fruit, like raspberries and strawberries, will of course be eaten with a spoon and fork or fork only. Grapes and cherries are eaten by hand, the stones or pips being returned to the plate inside the curved fingers.

Remarking on the food

Guests these days should forget all they have ever heard about 'It's rude to make remarks about food!', 'Do not mention what you eat', etc. That is all out of date. Hostesses are hurt and upset if they prepare an excellent meal and nobody comments on it. I have found that the only people who don't say how delicious my food is, are those who are too busy pretending they have better fare at home!

Whether the hostess has cooked the meal herself or has a cook, she always likes to be thanked. My daughter, who has a wonderful Italian chef, often takes her guests into the kitchen after dinner so that they can compliment him on the meal.

Chef was thrilled to meet the beautiful Countess of Dalkeith, but he was even more excited when his own Ambassador, the charming Count Zoppi, spoke to him at length in his own language.

Thanks

A guest on leaving should thank profusely for being entertained and must write a letter of thanks the following day. It is quite correct to mention in the letter how delicious the meal was and how charming or pretty the hostess looked. In fact, most hostesses are disappointed if there aren't two or three compliments in a 'bread and butter' letter.

Bringing a friend

It is wrong, except in special circumstances or because you know the host and hostess very well, to ask whether you may bring someone else to a party.

I have never given a big party without being infuriated by people who say: 'Aggie Smith, who knew you twenty years ago, would love to see you again; do you mind if I bring her?' or, 'My aunt and two cousins will be staying with me. I know you won't mind their coming with me.'

The natural answer is that you mind very much, especially when, in the case of garden parties or balls, one is paying caterers at so much per head. But very few hosts are brave

BRINGING A FRIEND

enough to say no; so Aggie, Auntie and Uncle Tom Cobley and all turn up for a free entertainment.

Balls

Young men who are taken in dinner parties to balls given by debutantes should dance at least once with the girls in the party. They must also ask the debutante for whom the ball is being given for a dance and, if they have really good manners, the hostess.

They must write and thank both their dinner party hostess and the hostess who has given the ball. The same applies to the girls.

Telephone calls

Telephone calls in other people's houses must always be paid for and, when making the call, be careful to ask how much it is.

Stamps

When going away always take your own stamps with you. If you do ask your hostess for one you will, of course, pay for it, but it is so annoying for her to have to provide her guests with the stamps she has bought for her own letters.

Writing paper

If staying with friends for a long time or if you have to write an abnormal number of letters it is polite to take your own writing paper and envelopes.

Gifts

A gift of flowers, chocolates or a book for your host is always greatly appreciated and starts a visit off on a very happy basis. Far too many people stay away and forget that entertaining, even in a small way, costs money. Men who drink a lot should, unless their host is a wealthy man, take a bottle of whisky, gin or brandy with them. No one is likely to be offended.

Complaints

Do be appreciative. Don't take everything for granted. Flowers in your bedroom, a comfortable bed, good food and a pretty hostess should all be the subject of a pretty speech—that is if you want to be asked again.

Tipping

In a home where there are servants it is customary for a man to tip the butler and the women the housemaid. The amounts will depend on the age and status of the guests and the length of the stay, but will probably range from 5/- to £1.

Refusing drink

If, on principle, you do not drink wine, then no one will criticise you for being an abstainer

—at least no one of breeding. In refusing wine —or any other alcoholic drink—say, quietly and firmly 'No, thank you, I don't drink alcohol', and leave it at that. Avoid any suggestion of smugness or superiority and do not go into any details of the whys and the wherefores.

There is nothing more boring than the teetotaller on his hobby-horse—unless it is the health crank who tries, very erroneously, to prove that alcohol is rank poison.

Drunkenness

Even if you have no dislike of wines and spirits and no ethical objection to them, refrain from them if you have a light head. Intoxication is neither amusing nor mannerly. It is objectionable and embarrassing. Once again, do not go into explanations of how you get 'tight' and say the most outrageous things after one glass of sherry. Say 'no' and leave it at that.

In this regard even those who like to boast of their hard heads should drink less than they imagine they can. In the first place it is bad manners to drink, rather than sip, during a meal, and in the second it is a doubtful compliment to the host on the choice of his drink to make him incur needless expense in keeping up with your thirst.

Empty glasses

A good host will fill, or replenish, or have a servant replenish, your glass when it is empty. Therefore always leave at least a third of the glass untouched until the end of the course or the meal. Remember that at formal or even informal functions there may be the loyal toast or several toasts to be drunk.

It is embarrassing as well as rude to have to stand up and pretend to drink the toast from an empty glass.

INTOXICATION IS NEITHER AMUSING NOR
MANNERLY

Beer

At luncheon in a country house as in a roadside inn most men drink England's traditional brew.

At lunch it is usual, therefore, to offer beer to the male guests and wine to the females.

I must finish this chapter with my favourite epitaph:

'Here lie I and my two daughters,
Dead from drinking Cheltenham's waters.
If we had stuck to Epsom Salts,
We shouldn't be lying in these 'ere vaults.'

Eight

MANNERS ON THE MOVE

Prestige in public

One of the most certain ways of knowing whether good manners are a veneer or a genuine characteristic is to watch how persons behave when they are away from home and their own environment.

Not long ago the Government felt it necessary to point out that the good name and even the industrial prosperity of the country were being jeopardised by the slovenly manner in which some British tourists behaved abroad.

The American State Department has also been so worried by the bad manners of many of its nationals in all parts of the world that booklets on etiquette have been issued and publicity campaigns introduced to remedy matters.

Probably good manners are more important away from home than at any other time, because, however unimportant one may be, in trains and aircraft and more particularly in hotels, one becomes a public figure and an ambassador for one's country.

I am often appalled by my fellow countrymen. In France I saw four young men who had wined too well, try to butt in on a respectable family party. They asked the women to dance and were rude when they refused.

In India Europeans often behave in a manner which makes one hot and cold with embarrassment. The Indians have an exquisite courtesy due to their centuries-old good breeding, and I have seen them pretend not to understand when Britishers talked loudly and aggressively about 'blacks' and 'niggers' in their presence.

Manners abroad

This question of manners abroad is becoming more and more important as the popularity of overseas holidays increases. Good behaviour has become a matter of national prestige as well as personal reputation.

On the whole British people are well liked because most behave decently, but just a few can do us as a nation a lot of harm. Tens of thousands of schoolchildren go in parties to Belgium, France, Switzerland and Italy. Most behave well and are adequately supervised. A few get out of hand—and these are the ones who get British youngsters a bad name with hotel keepers, police and transport authorities.

Nor are children travelling abroad in groups the only offenders. Sometimes the behaviour of children accompanying their parents is appalling. One sees in hotels all too obvious proof of the lack of discipline that exists at home. This is bad enough in a British restaurant or hotel but abroad the contrast with foreign children makes it infinitely worse.

The people of Europe apparently love children much more than we do, and there is

A FEW GET OUT OF HAND ...

very little of that banishing them from the adult's table which we practise. But the privilege of sharing most of the adult activities on holiday involves a childish duty too—a duty to behave. Consequently one sees quite tiny children sitting quietly at the meal table, respecting the public rooms as a place they share with others and not as their personal nursery, showing deference to adults in lifts, doorways and so on.

By contrast British children are allowed to squirm in their seats and get down half-way through the unaccustomedly long meal. They rampage around the hotel, push their way in front of adults and make thorough nuisances of themselves.

It gives a bad impression to expect continental hoteliers to do more for children than is their custom. There are many differences from British hotels and it is bad manners to demand the same sort of service and complain when it is not forthcoming.

Continental hoteliers are realists. They have long ago discovered that a boy or girl in the early teens causes more trouble through untidiness in the bedroom and can eat as much as or more than most adults. It should not, therefore, be expected that reductions in prices are automatically given, especially when the average British tourist expresses horror at the common continental practice of quite grown-up children sharing the parental bedroom, usually with some sort of screen.

Equally, in the case of young children, do not demonstrate your lack of experience in continental customs and expect half-size meals at half price, with the evening meal served early. Nor will the overworked staff regard baby-sitting as a normal part of their duties.

Dictatorial instructions about children's matters, as about all others, will get you nowhere unless you are staying in a 'super-luxe' establishment where additions to the bill mollify all trouble imposed on the management. But friendliness and polite requests will work miracles. If there is one characteristic common to foreigners from Moscow to Madrid it is the adoration of children—well brought-up children.

If a mother approaches the chambermaid as a woman who probably has children of her own or certainly dreams of the day when she will, instead of issuing lofty orders in the alleged style of a Georgian duchess on the Grand Tour, she will find she can get virtually anything she wants done on behalf of her children. There will be none of that sullen 'It's not my job and anyway I'm off duty at seven' one gets in Britain.

Similarly, at meal-times, the waiter, approached as a member of the parents' club and not as a paid lackey, will quickly volunteer to provide just the sort of food the children seem to like.

Courtesy :an inborn virtue of the Latin races; it is a tourist attraction and a legally enforced virtue in the harder-headed nations to the North. Either way the infringements of convention practised by tourists will be overlooked and partially forgiven, though ill feeling will inevitably remain.

The consequence is that some British visitors, warned of this or that law and this or that custom, duly ignore them and then report that they were legends because no policeman arrested them. They were probably too thick-skinned to notice that they were gently ostracised and got rather bad service, plus some overcharging.

When abroad one should lean over backwards to observe the spirit as well as the letter of the local laws to a far greater extent than in Britain. Here minor infringements of the traffic regulations are — perhaps unfortunately — practised because the police do not take action over them.

But though one may get away with 33 miles per hour in a built-up area in Britain there is no excuse to ignore speed limits on the Continent where, in any case, the restrictions are enforced with mathematical precision against local inhabitants.

In the same way it may be condoned in Britain to use an exit as an entrance or an entrance as an exit, but this is no reason to misinterpret 'eingang' and 'entrée' just to indicate one's superiority to rules.

At most national boundaries a welcome booklet is handed to the tourist or there are multilingual notices explaining the principal rules so that all may enjoy life without interfering with the rights of others.

Generally speaking, what is good behaviour in one country will be so regarded in another, and minor discrepancies will be forgiven by the obvious attempt to be correct. Specifically, here are some of the more general and widespread rules in countries which tourists are likely to visit.

... TO USE AN EXIT AS AN ENTRANCE

France and the Benelux countries

At passport control details may be demanded on a card. It is not clever to fill in the required facts in a fictional manner. These cards often enable the police to trace visitors quickly when they are needed back home. In any event it is the law that they should be filled in accurately.

Attempts at amateur smuggling are both rude and unwise. Rarely will any charge be made on normal goods willingly declared. Bluffing and threats to ring the British Ambassador will not intimidate the officials nor avail much if you are in the wrong.

In hotels and restaurants it is pleasanter and more reasonable to regard the management as honest until proved otherwise. The old stories of everyone catering for visitors being robbers and vultures applies no more abroad than here. Haggling over room costs at the outset may produce a cheaper room—and certainly worse service. Haggling afterwards is futile and bad manners.

Normal requests for extra blankets, pillows or attention to the water supply will be met, and invariably the local tourist office will investigate complaints if facilities are poorer than the claims put forward for them.

It is better to put a serious complaint to the authorities, who are there to deal with them, than to start a rumpus in front of other guests.

But if you must make complaints remember that shouting does not assist foreigners to understand your rude English any better.

Courtesy to everyone is far better observed in Europe than in Britain. To women it is beyond comparison. Age automatically attracts politeness from youth. These factors mean more than nationality, class or personality. A town's richest business man will raise his hat to the beggar woman selling matches, and the smallest child will regard a word from an old man as a privilege.

Common errors of good behaviour I have noted among British tourists abroad include:

France

Smoking in cinemas and theatres.

Wearing sports clothes or abbreviated sun-bathing attire in restaurants and hotels.

Regarding churches and abbeys as museums instead of living places of worship where propriety and quiet are essential. (*Note*. Women should always cover their heads in a Catholic Church.)

Crossing roads in defiance of point duty police.

Talking loudly and making a noise either very late or early in the hotel.

Men not removing their hats in a lift when ladies are present and not letting a lady leave first.

Not saying 'Madame' and 'Monsieur' as the French do to everyone including shop assistants, bus conductors and flower-sellers.

Not tipping the attendant who shows you into your seat at a cinema and theatre, as is the custom.

Not tipping the wine waiter in restaurants, as is the custom.

Switzerland

Ignoring the strict rules in most areas about abbreviated costume in public places—for instance, on lake steamers and in the streets it is usually forbidden for a man to appear without a shirt.

Smoking in buses and in non-smoking compartments in trains.

Throwing away litter in the street and stations. (*Note.* The Swiss are fanatically clean.)

Italy

Visiting churches in abbreviated costume and, in the case of women, without a head covering and with bare arms.

Assuming that every man who smiles happily is attempting seduction or rape.

Spain

Wearing bikinis on the beach, or beach sun-bathing costumes away from the beaches.

Unseemly dress and behaviour in churches.

Making disparaging remarks about the Franco régime or generally criticising the backwardness of the country and its people.

Men not taking off their hats when religious processions go by.

Being offensive at Bullfights. If you aren't prepared to grit your teeth and bear it—don't go.

NO BIKINIS ON SPANISH BEACHES

Denmark

Making rude remarks about the bed coverings which are blankets buttoned into clean sheets, making a kind of eiderdown, but which cannot be tucked in. Just ask pleasantly for an extra blanket and tuck that in over it— you will be quite comfortable. (*Note*. This type of bed-covering is found in most Scandinavian countries).

Germany and Austria

Making loud asides about the Nazi régime, air raids damage and the alleged Hun mentality. (Most Germans speak and understand English).

Note. In none of these countries should men on holiday sit down to meals with their coats off and wearing braces, nor is it funny or clever to make fun of, or to be too familiar with, the waitress.

COURTESY WHEN TRAVELLING

On the road

Courtesy on the road is possibly a classic example where good manners pay the biggest dividends of all—freedom from injury and death. Regrettably there are too many people who, once they are behind a steering wheel, lose all sense of courtesy.

The drivers of big lorries have extraordinarily

good manners; they wave one on, keep to the side of the road and in too many instances 'show up' the private motorist.

In England motorists are furious when you hoot at them. In France and Italy you will be in trouble if you don't. Personally, if a car or a lorry lets me pass I always wave my hand to say 'thank you'.

On the railway

In railway trains and aircraft we have all met men and women, well dressed and presumably also well educated, who smoke in non-smoking compartments, put the window up or down without consideration for the other passengers, and seem to think that parcels, newspapers and their suitcases are entitled to a seat to themselves.

It is important to remember that people are often confused and agitated at railway stations. The noise of the engine, the crowds, the fear of missing their train all combine to make them edgy, so they snap and snarl. Think of this or you will find yourself being snappy!

Do be pleasant and friendly to people in railway carriages. There is no need to talk on a long journey but only in Britain could travellers journey from London to Land's End or Glasgow and never say a word because they haven't been introduced.

There is a story of a jolly commercial traveller who got into a compartment with only one lady in it. He passed the time of day and was rewarded with an averted head and pressed lips. Three or four times he tried to be friendly, only to be received in silence until at last he gave it up and went to sleep.

He awoke an hour or so later and saw that the train was running into his station. Opposite him was his proud and silent companion, fast asleep. She awoke as he picked up his bag and opened the door.

'Good-bye,' he said with a smile. 'You may not wish to speak to me but I shall always remember we have slept together!'

I always talk to people in railway carriages and everywhere else because I like people. I once received a proposal of marriage from a complete stranger with whom I had talked between London and Cardiff. And also one from a millionaire who carried my dressing case from a cross-Channel steamer into the train waiting at Dover.

In the air

At airports one is faced with the embarrassment of pushing and shoving one's way on to the aeroplane in order to get the seat one prefers, or behaving in a dignified manner and getting what is left. I have protested again and again to B.O.A.C. and B.E.A. and at last one is able to book if one travels first class and on long distance flights.

It would be quite easy for all air companies to arrange that seats booked a fortnight before the flight could be chosen like theatre seats. It will come eventually, but in the meantime we have the deplorable exhibition of women in mink and wealthy industrialists using their elbows.

A DEPLORABLE EXHIBITION

As one cannot tip the stewardess on an airliner I always shake hands with her and say 'thank you' as she waits at the top of the gangway to see you off the plane. Usually to each passenger she says: 'Good-bye. I hope you had a pleasant journey, Sir (or Madam).

It is shameful how many people refuse to answer or mutter something indistinct.

Decent behaviour while on the move is subjected to little rigid convention. All that one needs is a modicum of common sense plus a policy of 'Do as you would be done by'.

At the hotel

On reaching a hotel the first rule which has to be observed concerns the signing of the register. A glance at any hotel register will invariably indicate on a single page how many people err in this regard. What the hotel requires is the guest's name. A man, therefore, should write his usual signature, although perhaps a little more decipherably than normal.

If his wife is accompanying him, he signs on her behalf as well—and writes 'Mr and Mrs J. B. Smith'.

If children in their teens are with their parents, their christian names should be given —'Mr and Mrs J. B. Smith, Mary Smith and John Smith'.

It is wrong to put 'Mr and Mrs Smith and

family'. If the children are very small, one should write 'Mr and Mrs Smith, three children and Nurse'.

A woman staying by herself at an hotel will indicate her status by putting either Mrs or Miss in front of her initials and surname.

Manners in hotels

Any hotel servant can unfortunately recount all too many stories about the disgraceful behaviour of guests. Cheating and stealing occur in a manner which seems incomprehensible. Towels, ash-trays, lavatory paper, soap and even light bulbs are considered fair game, and in one hotel I know they had to be continually replacing the blankets.

The fact that one is paying for accommodation does not make it any the less necessary to behave as one would if one were a guest in the house of a lifelong friend or relative.

One should also behave with even more consideration for other people, because they are strangers. Rules about times and periods of baths, meals, radios in the bedrooms, quietness in the corridors and so on, are rightly observed by the well-mannered guest. If, by any chance, he considers there is too much regimentation about the place, he neither complains loudly to his fellow guests about it nor tries to improve the situation by infringing the rules.

Conversation with fellow guests

The British have a reputation for being stand-
offish as regards strangers. This is possibly
true, but it must be accepted as the conventional
behaviour. It is not our custom to get into
conversation with fellow guests too easily or
too quickly.

This may or may not be regrettable, but the
fact remains that very many people stay at
hotels for the purpose of living in peace and
comfort and so that they can be left to their
own devices. The coincidence of a number of
people living under the same roof is no reason
why any one of them should be compelled to
talk to another.

At the same time if one is in a hotel for a week
or so, I think it rude not to say 'good morning'
to the people you meet several times a day in
the lift, and be ready to talk to them should
they wish it.

Entertaining friends in an hotel

A guest who makes friends at an hotel or has
friends in from outside should never invite
them into the bedrooms. Apart from the
obvious moral factor that arises if either party
is single, the bedroom, unless there is a sitting-
room attached, must be regarded as a place in
which to rest and dress. It is not meant for
entertaining. All social occasions should be

confined to the public rooms and while most hotel managements have no objection whatever to people who are not guests at the hotel visiting friends who are, this privilege should never be abused.

Tipping

Tipping is often a bugbear even to people who have visited hotels on hundreds of occasions. An increasing number of hotels in this country and practically all of them abroad now have a service charge of 10 to $12\frac{1}{2}$ per cent which is added to the bill.

TIPPING IS OFTEN A BUGBEAR

Usually a guide book, tariff or a notice at the reception desk will indicate whether this service charge is in use or not. If in doubt, it is advisable to enquire about it when signing the register.

Whether a service charge applies or not, the porter who brings up the baggage expects a tip. It can be as low as 1/- if a single traveller is simply staying overnight and a maximum of 5/- is usual if the guest has a galaxy of cases and the hotel is an expensive one.

When a service charge is not made, then it is usual to tip rather above the 10 per cent. The more expensive the hotel, the higher the percentage for tips; but it would be an ostentatious place indeed where more than 15 per cent of the bill would have to be added for gratuities.

Working out the proportions is a matter for personal discrimination, and it should be done on a frank basis of thanks for services rendered rather than a timorous acceptance of blackmail.

Assuming that a couple has stayed at a moderately priced hotel for a week at a cost, including extras, of £36 for both, ten per cent of that comes to £3. 12s.—say £3. 15s. to obtain a round figure.

Of this sum £1. 5s. might go to the chambermaid, left on the dressing table on the morning of departure; £1. 5s. to the table waiter given at the end of the last meal; 10s. to the wine waiter as one leaves the restaurant for the last time, and 10s. to the porter as he bids the guests good-bye.

This leaves 5s. for anyone else who may have given service—a pageboy, night porter or garage attendant. If there is a head waiter in addition to the other two then the £1. 15s. allocated for the restaurant staff could be divided in the proportion of £1., 10s., and 5s.

Usually the proportion hardly matters as all the money will go into a 'tronc' and will be divided on some basis agreed to by the staff.

In most hotels the rule is that bills are paid weekly and in the same way tips are given weekly. Having worked out what $12^1/_2$ per cent —or whatever proportion one has decided on— comes to on the current week's bill, the sum should be divided among the servants who have helped to make your stay pleasant.

Whether or not there is a service charge, one always tips for special service such as a waiter who brings you drinks or mineral water late at night, and the chambermaid if she fills hot-water bottles, packs or unpacks.

Attitude to receptionists

It is all too common for people unaware of the proprieties of staying at hotels to give a gratuity to the man or girl at the desk when settling the bill. With the courtesy that is part of their job, they will probably accept it with a word of thanks; but at the same time it is in effect an insult to them because they are part of the management and do not rank among the servants of the hotel.

Pooling of tips

In virtually all hotels the written or unwritten law is that the staff in each section pool their gratuities. Thus, all the staff in the dining-room or working on its behalf will benefit from the tips you give to your own waiter. In the same way the chambermaids will share their gratuities with the women who clean the rooms and bathroom and probably with the boy who cleans the shoes.

It is therefore usually unnecessary to bother one's head because the chambermaid who has been so helpful or the waiter who was so attentive is nowhere to be found on the day one leaves.

No tips

The following are never tipped:
Pursers on ships.
Air hostesses and stewards on aeroplanes.
Reception clerks who show you to your room in an hotel.
Women's hairdressers who own their shops. (If you go to a special man regularly you give him a good present at Christmas).

220

To be tipped

Tips should always be given to the following:

Taximen, between 6d. and 1/- for short distances.

The doorkeeper who fetches you a taxi, between 6d. and 1/-

The cloakroom attendant who fetches a man his coat and hat, between 6d. and 1/-

The attendants in the lavatories both male and female, between 6d. and 1/-

Porters at stations—1/- for an ordinary suitcase or two and about another 6d. for every subsequent case.

In France, as I have already said, you always tip the attendant who shows you into your seat at a theatre, and the wine waiter in a restaurant.

Cooks

If I stay the weekend where the food is delicious and a great deal of trouble has been taken for my visit, I tip the cook. I go into the kitchen, shake her by the hand and thank her for the wonderful dishes she has prepared and give her £1 in an envelope. This is always done in France and it seems unfair that in England the cook, who provides so much for your enjoyment, is left out.

Chauffeurs

A chauffeur is tipped if he takes away your car at night and brings it round for you in the morning. 5/- to 10/- is usual.

Nine

THE ETIQUETTE OF ROMANCE

Times change customs and this certainly applies to love-making. Whether this is an improvement is questionable when we look at the large proportion of broken marriages among young people.

There is quite a lot to be said for parents having a much bigger say about their children's romantic activities than at present. Whatever our inclinations might suggest and whatever we are taught by the disciples of Freud, theory is not the same as practice.

However, the situation for most people in Britain today is that we implicitly believe love to be an accident. It comes through a chance meeting, the coincidence of working in the same office, or of being members of the same social club.

The young people insist, and have obtained the right to insist, that they shall be free to grasp their own happiness and, by implication, to make their own mistakes.

Legal aspects

However, the law in its wisdom still maintains

223

that young people cannot marry before they are sixteen and, in England and Wales, may not marry before they are twenty-one without the approval of their parents. The custom is therefore maintained of at least paying lip service to the suggestion that parents have the right to approve or disapprove of their children's marriage proposals.

Good manners safeguard love

Generally speaking, I believe that young people will not be involved in immorality or unsuitable love affairs if they have been brought up with high standards. Children with wise, understanding parents who have set a good example learn to think with their brains as well as feel with their hearts.

They recognise vulgarity, commonness of mind, deception and hypocrisy wherever they meet it.

Parents' attitude to their children's romances

How essential this training in childhood is will be realised when a son talks about his first girl friend or a daughter about her boy friend. It is very probable that the news will be quite unexpected and the person referred to will be unknown to the parents.

In other words, the beginning of the average romance takes place without the knowledge of the parents. It is therefore their preparatory

work, long before the age of potential indis-
cretion, which lays the foundation of the
proper attitude towards the opposite sex.

I remember some years ago talking to a
friend, when her small son came running in,
his eyes alight with excitement.

'Mummy! Mummy! Listen....' he cried,
and began a long and somewhat involved
story about the child next door.

'Oh, run along!' my friend said. 'I haven't
time to listen to that nonsense.'

A few weeks ago I asked my friend how her
son was doing in his new job.

'I've no idea,' she answered, and added with
bitterness, 'he never tells me anything.'

The lesson is obvious. To guide and lead
their children parents must gain their confidence
when they first begin to talk. A mother who
has listened to the worries and the difficulties
of school-days and been sympathetic to the
varying stages of hero-worship from the
'terror of the third form' to a passion for
Adam Faith, will automatically find herself
being told about that 'marvellous boy I met
last night' or 'that jolly pretty girl I met at
the office party.'

Just as secretiveness and deception are
examples of bad manners and bad behaviour,
so are intolerance and lack of understanding.
The well brought-up youngster of understanding parents is very unlikely to indulge in

a friendship of a clandestine nature and it is extremely unlikely that he will begin even the mildest of friendships with someone of whom he is ashamed.

Love interests

Children should be encouraged from an early age to talk about their friends and name them. To the question, 'Who are you meeting tonight?' it is bad manners to reply, 'A friend!'

Parents must show interest without excessive curiosity. It is difficult for them but they can easily antagonise their children at this most critical time in their lives.

'I never tell my parents anything about my young men,' a girl told me. 'How can I? They either jump to the conclusion that I'm engaged before the man has even proposed and say things to him which cover me with embarrassment. Or else they disapprove and make scenes when I propose to do nothing more drastic than accept an invitation to a dance or a cocktail party.'

Such parents punish themselves by their own stupidity.

Home influences

However slight the interest may appear to be, it is wise for parents to encourage their children to bring their friends home. If these occasions are arranged informally—such as suggesting that the man drops in for a glass of sherry before going to a dance or a cup of coffee after visiting a cinema or a theatre—there can be no question that the parents regard the friendship as a serious romance.

If such visits are encouraged, then the news of an eventual engagement cannot come as a surprise to anyone. And there is, of course, the advantage that the young man has made the acquaintance of his future in-laws, and a

PARENTS SHOULD ENCOURAGE THEIR CHIDREN
TO BRING THEIR FRIENDS HOME

girl finds it much less of an ordeal when she is taken to meet her fiancé's parents.

An evening out

A young man taking a girl out for the evening usually calls for her at her parents' house or flat. It is correct for her father or mother to offer a cocktail or sherry and to talk to him for about five or ten minutes.

The young man should take the girl home when the evening is over but he should not go into her house if there is any likelihood that her parents have gone to bed. And the girl should not invite him to come in.

Entertaining boy friends and girl friends

Thousands of young people, at Universities or in lodgings because their employment takes them away from home, are at some time or another faced with the problem of entertaining *à deux*.

When the problem was an informal party with half a dozen or so there was no difficulty; people just drifted in and the affair more or less ran itself, the food and drink being dependent principally on the resources of the host— and very possibly on the generosity of the guests.

Having one's boy friend or girl friend up to one's room is comparatively new in so far as it is no longer daring or improper. Most landladies appear to have dropped the policy of 'no visitors of the opposite sex' for one of 'no visitors after 11 p.m.'

The older generation must be realistic about this and accept that two young people who are not engaged, and may not even imagine themselves to be in love, regard it as perfectly conventional to spend the evening in a private room together.

This is understandable and, apart from the rather prurient forebodings of their elders, sensible. There cannot be parties in friends' rooms every night. Sitting in cafés and pubs becomes as boring—and expensive—as a constant round of cinemas.

If the underlying purpose is to seduce or be seduced obviously nothing written here will affect either host or guest in the slightest, but it would be unjust to deny the fresh and healthy attitude of the younger generation to their relationships with one another.' Come up and see my etchings' is as dead as straw boaters and stage-door mashers. 'Come up and listen to my new L.P.' means precisely what the words imply.

As a room in which someone eats, lives, works and sleeps represents the entire resources of a house, some little preparation is needed to make the occasion a success and to show those good manners which obviate a guest's embarrasment, not to mention the host's.

The place should be clean and tidy, with all evidence of washing, sleeping, and laundering hidden away. All those bright ideas in the women's magazines about cooking a memorable four-course dinner on a gas ring should be forgotten. Coffee and sandwiches, or some of the attractive made-up dishes sold ready-to-eat by delicatessen shops, with a few bottles of soft drinks, are all that is necessary.

There is an unwritten law—the emergence of etiquette for the 1960's—that alcohol is not provided at this sort of twosome party, unless it is a single bottle of innocuous and inexpensive white wine.

Few young people are artificially coy about washing and going to the lavatory. For those who are it is worth realising that to get the subject over with right from the start is the host's duty. 'The lavatory's along there and the bathroom's next to it', said in a matter-of-fact voice as the host leads his or her guest from the front door should dispose of the geographical problem.

The occasion is not the host's responsibility. Even modern youngsters can be annoyed and embarrassed by an artificial pause in the conversation with followed by 'er...I don't know whether you want.....'

The guest—or the host for that matter—should simply say 'excuse me for a moment', and walk out of the room.

The host should plan some kind of activity rather than believe that everything will be fine if 'we just talk'. If each finds the other entrancing then conversation will replace playing records, playing rummy, or going over last week's lecture notes or whatever the intended interest.

But people who merely like one another yet really have little in common will get on much better if there's something to do instead of discussing the weather, the future of humanity, or the cost of living. None of these topics can be relied on to fill more than twenty minutes of a three hour evening.

It is bad manners and bad policy to make these evenings longer than three hours at the most. If the guest drops in at, say, 7.30 p.m. then to go about 10 p.m. will be appropriate, and the host should not press him or her to stay longer.

The matter of contributing to these occasions can be a delicate one if there is not preliminary frankness on either side.

A lot depends on the financial state of both parties. Two students, at college on State grants, will know almost to a nicety how much each has to spend on recreation. The guest will naturally be alarmed if the host has obviously spent beyond his or her budget. There is also the topsy-turvy situation where a girl secretary is earning far more than her friend, who is an apprentice or student.

Where the host is known to have to worry about money matters a modest contribution to the evening—say some drink, fruit or chocolates—which can be mutually shared, cannot come amiss. A girl should be cautiously modest in her contribution, for the male is sensitive about his inability to spend money on a female, even in these modern times. If he earns as much as or more than his guest then the wisest policy is no contribution at all.

If the host is a girl and she is known to be earning a good salary and rather proud of her independence, then her male guest will be wise to see that his gift is non-utilitarian and perhaps a little frivolous. He cannot go wrong with flowers.

This money business preoccupies innumerable young men who are at heart very old-fashioned and secretly dislike the widespread evidence of feminine equality.

On outings the girl would be wise to let her escort pay, being careful to choose inexpensive drinks and dishes, insisting that she prefers the stalls at the cinema or the gallery at the theatre. In fact she should lean over backwards not only to prove she is no gold-digger but also to avoid making her escort starve for the rest of the week, which he will do if he can— just to show off.

Many a girl has spoiled what she expected

to be a delightful friendship by insisting on sharing expenses or even pushing some money under or across the restaurant table. Equally, many a boy who greatly enjoyed a girl's company had to shy off simply because he couldn't afford the more and more frequent meetings.

The solution of this problem is entirely in the hands of the girl. With that frankness

HE CANNOT GO WRONG WITH FLOWERS

which is such a charming feature of the youth of today she can, after two or three outings, speak straight out, saying that although she enjoys the evenings together very much, it's unfair to go on in this way, and couldn't they come to some sensible understanding about finances?

That pleasant euphemism 'Dutch treat' is a nice way of broaching the subject of sharing expenses. If the idea is grudgingly accepted, the girl should be sure to be the junior partner in the arrangement by handing over her money to her escort so that he can appear to be paying for everything. This gentle hypocrisy mollifies the masculine embarrassment.

Young people being what they are, some of these companionships are likely to lead to romance, though unfortunately the romantic notions may be on one side only.

Remember that good manners have one principal object: to avoid hurting other people. If a girl or a man notices, to his or her consternation, that the person hitherto regarded as a delightful friend is spoiling things by getting morose and sentimental, the friendship should be broken as quickly, but as gently as possible.

Do not imagine that it is a phase that will pass. It may in time, but it will get a lot worse first. It is kinder to find a host of reasons and a dozen excuses for quickly ending the friendship if romance was the last thing expected or desired.

Permission for an engagement

Years ago a young man approached a girl's parents and requested permission to 'pay his respects' to her. This certainly doesn't apply today; but if two young people become engaged it is the man's duty, before anyone else is told, to meet his future in-laws and tell them how much he loves their daughter and how earnestly he hopes to make her happy. He should also be prepared to talk frankly about himself, his family and his job.

Engagement letter

If, as often happens, the parents of the girl live in a different part of the country, the young man should write to them. Here is the sort of letter he should send:

Dear Mr and Mrs Bolton,

Doreen will have told you that she has promised to marry me. We are terribly happy and I know I am the luckiest man in the world to have won someone as sweet as Doreen. I only hope you will not be too disappointed by her choice but I promise you that I will do all in my power to make her happy.

I am so looking forward to meeting you both as Doreen has told me so much about you and I know what a devoted family you are.

I am hoping to get a weekend off next month when perhaps you could come to London to meet my parents.

With all best wishes,
Yours sincerely,

Precedence of family meetings

Of the two meetings of the young couple with the parents concerned, that of the girl's parents should come before that of the young man's parents.

It is then the duty of the man's father or mother to write an informal and friendly letter to the girl's parents saying how delighted they are about the engagement.

This letter should be answered promptly in terms of the same kind and should also contain suggestions for a date when all the parties concerned can get to know one another.

Which family finally acts as host for this first meeting is not really of great social consequence and depends largely on convenience, but the first move should come from the parents of the young man.

Notifying relations

The first thing to be done immediately a girl and a young man have decided to get married and told their respective fathers and mothers is to notify all their other relatives. They should never hear about the engagement from a third party or see it announced in the newspapers. They should also be told before the girl wears her engagement ring.

All relatives and close friends must be told by the parents of 'the happy couple' and only when they are quite sure that everyone connected with the family knows what is happening can the engagement be made public.

BUYING THE ENGAGEMENT RING

Engagement ring

An engagement ring is usually the personal choice of the bride-to-be unless there is a traditional ring in the family or the bride-groom's mother gives her son some of her own jewels. Many brides today are wise enough not to insist on diamonds unless their future husband is very rich. Aquamarines, pale sapphires and topaz make lovely rings and one can have a beautiful large stone for a relatively low cost.

The only stones not usually used for engagement rings—because of superstition—are opals, which are supposed to bring bad luck, and pearls, which mean tears.

Engagement announcements

There is a correct wording for the announcement of an engagement which should always be followed. It is usually put in *The Times* and *The Daily Telegraph* and paid for by the bride's parents.

Announcements in these newspapers will only be accepted in writing with a covering letter signed by one of the parents. The cost in *The Times* is 63/- for three lines and 21/- for each additional line, and in *The Daily Telegraph*, five lines cost 87/6d. and each additional line 17/6d.

The announcement should read as follows:

MR A. J. HARROW
AND MISS P. J. WATKINS

The engagement is announced between Arthur James, only son of Major R. N. Harrow, M.C., and Mrs Harrow of Bolton Lodge, Puddleford, Gloucestershire, and Phillipa Joan, eldest daughter of Mr Harold Watkins and Mrs Watkins, of Woodbury, Hadley Wood, Hertfordshire.

If the bride is a widow the announcement then should read:

MR G. H. HENDERSON
AND MRS R. P. BRIGHT

The engagement is announced and the marriage will take place quietly between Geoffrey, son of Sir George Henderson and Lady Henderson, of 25, Brompton Square, S.W.1. and Rose Pamela, of Birch Cottage, Maybury, Dorset, widow of Brigadier W. D. Bright, D.S.O., of the Hertfordshire Regiment, and daughter of the late Canon S. Phillips and Mrs Phillips.

Period of engagement

The modern tendency is for short engagements, and the majority of weddings seem to take place within three or four months of the announcement.

This allows time for a girl to collect her trousseau, for the wedding arrangements to be made, and, more important, for a home to be found.

Nowadays, the need to select a time of year which will yield the greatest possible advantage from tax rebate is also a consideration to many couples.

Behaviour of engaged couples

The conventions as regards the behaviour of engaged couples do exist although unfortunately they are too often ignored.

A couple of generations ago an engaged girl of good class would never be seen in public with her fiancé except with a chaperone. After the First World War this stricture eased and—as today—engaged couples could go everywhere unescorted. But there should be no question of their staying away without there being a married woman in the house as chaperone.

Engaged couples should not kiss and cuddle each other passionately in public. It is embarrassing for other people and takes the fine edge off their own emotions.

A man should, however, always kiss his fiancée on arrival and departure, whoever else is present and wherever they may be.

Weekends and holidays

The practice of engaged couples, or for that matter, a number of young people who are just friends, going off for weekends and summer holidays without supervision is not really approved even by the most tolerant sections of society.

It is understandable that two people who are going to be married will wish to spend their weekends and their holidays together, but a married couple, or an older relative should accompany them if they are staying in an hotel.

Breaking off an engagement

Sometimes engagements have to be broken off. However regrettable, the parents of the estranged couple should not attempt to interfere once it is obvious that one or both of the parties have made up their minds. It is always disturbing and can often be a heart-breaking occurrence. Parents' first duty lies in helping bygones to be bygones by showing sympathy and understanding. Relatives and friends of the couple should not make enquiries as to the reasons.

One or other has obviously been jilted, but it is kinder to believe that the engagement has been broken off by mutual consent. If an engagement announcement has appeared in the newspapers then another announcement should be inserted exactly as follows:

CAPT. J. A. SIMPSON
AND MISS P. D. CHATTER
The marriage arranged between Captain J. A. Simpson and Miss P. D. Chatter will not now take place.

Any wedding presents already received should, of course, be returned immediately with a short letter of explanation.

Wedding presents

These must be thanked for as soon as possible after they arrive. The bride, who has always the greater number, writes to her friends; but where they are mutual, she must be careful to put—'John and I are simply delighted with your lovely present.'

If presents are shown after the wedding ceremony, it is very important to keep them carefully packed with the card showing the donor. People are very offended if, having given the bride and bridegroom a charming gift, their name has been lost.

Bachelor parties

It used to be traditional for a bridegroom to give a 'stag' party for his friends the night before his wedding. Fortunately this ridiculous custom is now completely out of date. If the prospective groom does give a party it is at least a week before the marriage ceremony. On the eve of his wedding, if he loves his future wife, he goes to bed early.

Bachelor parties are for only the closest friends of the bridegroom and if they are given

in an hotel they take place in a private room.
A well-chosen dinner and equally good wines
to go with it should be selected.

... SIMPLY DELIGHTED WITH YOUR LOVELY
PRESENT

243

Ten

MANNERS MAKYTH MARRIAGE

Legal and conventional aspects

A marriage is a legal contract, and there are formalities which must be observed by law as well as those encouraged by convention.

There are considerable differences between the marriage laws of England and Wales and those of Scotland. For this reason the position will be treated separately.

Banns

Under the Marriage Act of 1949 marriage in England by Banns demands audible publication of the banns during the morning service on three Sundays preceding the ceremony or, if there is no morning service, during the evening service. If the parties live in different parishes, the banns must be published in the churches of both parishes.

An important and sometimes advantageous change is that the wedding may take place in the church which is the usual place of worship of either of the persons to be married.

Thus, everyone who has made a practice of

244

attending services in a church outside his own parish can be married in that church, provided the banns are published in that church as well as in the other two. This privilege does not apply to Wales.

If, for some reason, a wedding has to be postponed at the last moment, the banns have to be republished after a lapse of three months.

Types of licence

There are two licences appertaining to marriage in the Church of England. Both are available without the necessity of publishing banns.

Common licence

A Common Licence is granted by the Archbishops, Bishops and Bishops through their Surrogates for marriage in any church licensed for marriages. It may be obtained from the Master of the Faculties, Faculty Office, The Sanctuary, Westminster S.W.1., for use in religious buildings throughout England and Wales. It can also be granted by Bishop's Diocesan Registry in the appropriate area where one or both parties are living. In the latter case the licences apply only to the diocese in which they are issued.

Applications, in person or by letter, must be made by one of the parties to be married. Relatives and friends are not permitted to give instructions for the issue of a licence. The cost varies according to the diocese but is usually between £1. 10s. and £2. 15s.

The stipulations to be fulfilled before a Common Licence is issued are:

1. An affidavit is sworn that there is no legal impediment to the marriage.
2. That the church proposed for the wedding is in the parish of the ecclesiastical district where one or both parties have resided for a minimum of fifteen days or that the proposed church is the usual place of worship of one of the persons to be married.

The Common licence is valid on the day of issue and remains in force for three months.

Special licence

A Special Licence is granted only by the Archbishop of Canterbury. It enables a marriage to be solemnised in any church at any time. Applications are dealt with by the Faculty Office (see address above), but a Special Licence is not lightly granted. There must be a very good reason for it.

Marriage by certificate

Marriage by Superintendent Registrar's Certificate: it is possible for a marriage to take place in church without the reading of banns or the use of the licences mentioned above by obtaining a Superintendent Registrar's Certificate.

It necessitates the approval of the incumbent of the church chosen for the wedding and he is not forced to give it. The situation arises only in rather unusual circumstances such as the foreign birth and possibly different Christian sect of one of the parties; but for most marriages this method is pointless.

Civil marriages

Marriages under a Superintendent Registrar's Certificate—civil marriages—can, of course, also be solemnised in religious buildings other than a Church of England.

These marriages take place in a registered building, such as a nonconformist church or chapel, the Meeting House of the Society of Friends (Quakers), in a synagogue, in a Church of England as explained in the preceding section, or in a registry office.

There are two forms of marriage under a Superintendent Registrar's Certificate. The first, without licence, demands that both parties reside in the same registration district for a minimum of seven days before notice is given, or if they reside in different districts that both have resided in those districts for a minimum of seven days, and that notice is given to the registrars of both districts.

The second, without licence, demands notice of intending marriage from only one party (either man or woman) who must have resided in the district for a minimum of fifteen days prior to the notice. The other party may be residing anywhere in England and Wales, but not in Scotland or abroad.

The notice in either case gives details of names, personal status (single, widowed, divorced), occupation, length of and place of residence, and place of the intended marriage.

The Certificate without Licence is issued twenty-one days after notice is given; the Certificate with Licence is issued after the lapse of one complete weekday.

MARRIAGE IN A REGISTRY OFFICE

The Certificate without Licence is displayed so that the public may see it; that with Licence is not so displayed.

Registrars' Certificates are valid for three months from the date of entry on the notice.

Times for weddings

Marriages in a registered building or a registry office must be in the presence of an authorised person, take place between 8 a.m. and 6 p.m. in the presence of two or more witnesses and with the doors open.

A religious ceremony is not permitted in a registry office, but a subsequent religious ceremony in a church or a religious building is allowed.

Jews may be married in a synagogue or a private house at any hour.

Scottish marriages

Marriages in Scotland may be regular or irregular, though the former will obviously be the only one of interest to those intending to wed.

Marriage in Scotland is simpler and cheaper. Any Minister of any denomination is regarded as a Minister of religion able to perform the marriage ceremony. There is no legal form of marriage, stipulated place, or forbidden time of the day.

Residence of one or both parties in the district must be a minimum of fifteen days, and whereas in a strict conception of the law the calling of banns on three occasions is needed, in fact by custom once on a Sunday is sufficient. A notice posted up at the Registrar's office for seven days is equivalent to the calling of banns.

The certificate issued after either of these methods costs only half-a-crown, and the marriage may take place. In exceptional circumstances the local Sheriff can issue a marriage licence without the banns or notice.

The Scottish irregular marriage, as a matter of interest, is by a law of 1939 recognised when a couple have lived together so that by repute and habit they are recognised as man and wife. Such irregular marriages can be registered.

Marriages between English and other persons

Marriages where one party resides in Scotland or Northern Ireland involve only slight differences. In Scotland the party living there has either to apply to the Clerk of Session or the local Registrar to publish banns or give notice, with proof of a minimum of fifteen days' residence.

In Northern Ireland the minimum residential period is seven days and the notice is given to the District Registrar.

Because of the time factor, marriage under a Superintendent Registrar's Certificate with Licence (i.e. so that the wedding can take place a day after notice is given) is not possible when one party is a resident of Scotland or Northern Ireland.

Marriage of minors

The principal difference between Scottish and English and Welsh marriages concerns minors.

In Scotland no consent of parents or guardians is necessary for minors over sixteen.

In England and Wales, of course, such permission is necessary, and it is worth noting that if both parents are living both must give consent. Insanity of a sole surviving parent dispenses with the need for consent. The Courts may give consent to the marriage of a minor despite the refusal of parents or guardians.

The prohibited degrees of marriage are, by civil law, now considerably relaxed. Civil marriage is, by the Act of 1949, permitted with:

Deceased wife's sister
Deceased brother's widow
Deceased wife's brother's daughter
Deceased wife's sister's daughter
Father's deceased brother's widow
Mother's deceased brother's widow
Deceased wife's father's sister
Deceased wife's mother's sister
Brother's deceased son's widow
Sister's deceased son's widow

Clergymen are not compelled to solemnise such marriages though they are authorised to allow a church to be used for such weddings presided over by another Minister.

Church weddings

Even if as a nation we are not church-goers, the majority of weddings still take place in a religious building. It will be seen that regulations to a great extent control the church where the wedding must take place, and if for some romantic or social reason it is desired to go to a church which is not the parish church of either party, then it will be necessary regularly to worship there and to prove the fact.

Preparatory moves

If parents of the engaged couple are regular church-goers, there will be no problem about making the preliminary enquiries. If they are not, there need be little embarrassment. With a few exceptions, clergymen are aware of their duty to bless all marriages and most are happy that even non church-goers wish a religious ceremony at this important stage of their lives.

A letter from the prospective bridegroom asking for an appointment to discuss the proposed marriage should be sent to the incumbent. It should be friendly, and should enquire rather than demand.

Upon being given an appointment to meet the incumbent both parties to the engagement should attend to talk matters over.

Time of the wedding

The time for the marriage depends on many factors. As indicated, it may legally take place at any hour between 8 a.m. and 6 p.m., and clergymen in populous parishes in the seasons favoured for marriages no doubt wish that people would utilise to the maximum the variety of times available.

However, given the sense to have made application well in advance of the three weeks needed for the banns, most couples will select some time between 11 a.m. and 3 p.m.

Morning and afternoon weddings

A wedding before noon is inevitably more expensive because it means a luncheon party. Against the disadvantage of this there is the boon for the newly-weds that they can reach their honeymoon address, even if it entails a long flight or a car journey, at a reasonable time.

The afternoon wedding, with its reception afterwards at which champagne and the cake are really the only costly factors, can mean a terrible rush for the bride and bridegroom.

Society weddings are nearly always in the afternoon owing to the very large number of guests who have to be invited to the reception.

Wedding invitations

When the details of the wedding have been settled, the invitations can be sent out. They should be posted three weeks prior to the ceremony. Printers and stationers will often do their utmost to persuade customers to have the invitations printed in silver on heavy cards, with bells and other embellishments. The correct type of invitation is shown on Page 114.

Invitations to quiet weddings

If the wedding is to be a quiet one, as is essential if there has been a death among the close relatives of the bridal couple within the past three months, the invitations are usually only to the church. These can be written by the bride's mother.

Such letters are not copies of the printed invitation but are written as friendly letters though, of course, giving all the necessary details.

Replies

Replies to a wedding invitation should be sent without delay out of consideration for the bride's parents making the arrangements. If it has been a formal invitation, then it is answered formally in the third person. If it has been a personal letter, then, of course, the personal style is followed in the reply.

The bride's parents send out all the invitations and the parents of the bridegroom give them a list of those they want invited.

Bridal dress

There is an old jingle which says:

> Married in Blue
> Her Love will be true,
> Married in White
> She has chosen aright,
> Married in Yellow
> She'll be ashamed of the fellow,
> Married in Red
> She'll wish herself dead,
> Married in Black
> She'll wish herself back,
> Married in Grey
> She'll travel far away,
> Married in Pink
> All her troubles will sink,
> Married in Green
> She'll be ashamed to be seen.

Every bride knows that she must wear 'something old, something new; something borrowed, something blue' on what is the most exciting, magical and lovely day of her life.

Rehearsal

In the case of a large wedding with bridesmaids

and pages, a rehearsal is really essential. It is most important to arrange where the bridesmaids shall stand when the bride and bridegroom move up to the altar steps. Also, if the pages are very young, it is best for them to sit during this part of the service, otherwise they fidget.

The service

In all but the very quietest weddings music is essential. It may mean merely the engagement of the organist; but if there are to be hymns, then the choir will also be needed. The parish priest will explain about the fees and so on at the preliminary interview. It is wise to talk over the music in some detail as a favourite hymn may not be well known to the choir and organist, and they will need time to rehearse it.

A printed form of service is usual because wedding guests do not bring prayer and hymn books with them. The wording, style and layout should be gone over very carefully with the church incumbent before printing is put in hand. These forms of service are handed out at the door by the ushers or placed in position in the pews.

Service papers

They should be a plain folder size and printed in black. It used to be wrong to include any decoration but now it is quite correct to have the bride and bridegroom's initials on the outside.

Ushers

Ushers are usually all chosen by the bridegroom and are his closest friends and relations. They greet each guest at the door and ask, 'Bride or Bridegroom?' They carry a list of relations and important guests and it is far easier if these people are definitely allotted places beforehand, with name cards in the pews.

The bride's friends sit on the left-hand side, the bridegroom's on the right.

Time of bridegroom's arrival

The bridegroom should arrive, with his best man, at the church a quarter of an hour before the bride is expected. He goes into the vestry and notifies the clergyman that he is present.

Bride's arrival

The bride arrives in a car alone with her father or whoever is giving her away. It is bad manners for her to be more than a minute or two late. There should be someone ready to arrange her train, if she has one, and her veil. Bridesmaids wait by the door in the correct order in which they follow her up the aisle. In some churches, the verger precedes the bride up the church.

The bride walks up the aisle holding her father's right arm and comes down on her husband's right arm so as to be on the left-hand side of the church where all her friends are sitting.

Bridegroom's delay

If by an unfortunate occurrence the bridegroom is late, the bride should wait quietly and composedly. She should not talk and she should in no way appear agitated.

Just cause or impediment?

If someone replies to the clergyman when, during the marriage service, he asks anyone to speak 'who can show just cause or impediment' why the marriage cannot take place, the bride and bridegroom should not turn round. The clergyman will tell them what to do. The members of the congregation should also be restrained and quiet.

During a big society wedding a few years ago at which I was present, a person with no authority or excuse made a commotion. The clergyman and the bride and bridegroom knew this might happen but the congregation had not been informed and their behaviour was excellent. Nobody stared, turned round or whispered and the ushers removed the objector from the church.

Signing the register

The parents of both bride and bridegroom, brothers, sisters and grandparents all sign the register. If Royalty is present, they also sign it.

Veils

The bride used always to have her face covered with a veil as a sign of purity. Today the veil is optional, but when the bride does wear one over her face, it is usually a detachable piece of tulle that, when removed in the vestry after the service, will not spoil the appearance of her head-dress or the rest of the veil hanging over her shoulders.

Bridal procession

After the bride and bridegroom, followed by the bridesmaids, have passed the first pews, the procession is joined by:

The Bride's father, giving his arm to the Bridegroom's mother.

The Bridegroom's father, giving his arm to the Bride's mother.

Grandparents, brothers and sisters and close relations from the first two pews on each side.

The rest of the guests in the church should wait until these have all passed by before leaving their pews.

Responsibility for expenses

The bridegroom is responsible for all expenses connected with the actual wedding ceremony. He pays for the licence (if one is needed), the fees to the officiating clergyman, bell ringers, organist, choir, verger and carpet.

Although the clergymen are paid, it is polite for the bride on her honeymoon to write him a letter of thanks. If the wedding has been fully choral it is also much appreciated if she writes to the organist.

While the bridegroom pays for the things I have mentioned, the actual transactions on the wedding day are carried out by the best man to whom the necessary money is given beforehand.

Wedding ring and flowers

The bridegroom buys the wedding ring and gives a present to the bride. He also pays for the bouquets carried by the bride and her bridesmaids and for his own, and the best man's buttonhole.

It is also a nice gesture for him to give a shoulder spray to his future mother-in-law as well as to his own mother.

Buttonholes

The bridegroom wears a white carnation as do the ushers. These must be single flowers *without* greenery or silver ends.

Gifts to bridesmaids

It is normal for the bridegroom to give some small gift, usually of jewellery, to each bridesmaid and a souvenir to any pages present. A vanity case with the bride's and bridegroom's initials on it can cost as little as 15s. The pages, traditionally, have cuff links, but small boys much prefer a toy or book.

Bride's parents' expenses

The expenses and work which fall on the bride's parents are as follows:

Preparing and paying for the engagement announcement.

Confirming the arrangements made for the wedding service by the engaged couple.

Preparing and addressing the wedding invitations.

Preparing and ordering the form of wedding service.

Choosing the bridesmaids (who pay for their own dresses).

Providing the bride's dress and trousseau.

Providing the flowers and decorations in the church.

Seating the most important guests in the front pews.

Organising the reception, with food, wine and

261

wedding cake etc.

Providing cars for the bridal party to go to the church; for the bridal couple, the bridesmaids, close relatives and guests without means of transport, from the church to the reception; for the newly married couple to start off on their honeymoon.

Speeches at the wedding reception

It is quite incorrect to have long speeches at a wedding. The only words which are really necessary are just before the bride cuts the cake, when the most distinguished guest present says: 'My Lords, Ladies and Gentlemen. I have much pleasure in proposing the toast of — the Bride and Bridegroom.'

Old friends, however, like to say a little more, but this should be cut to a maximum of two or three minutes.

Jokes about a future family—'the patter of little feet' etc. are bad taste. So are references to the bridegroom being 'a lad with the girls' and all that sort of thing.

When the bridegroom replies he says: 'On behalf of my wife and myself, thank you.'

Telegrams

These should never be read at the wedding. They are collected and given to the young couple to read on the journey when they go away.

Champagne

If the parents of the bride are not rich, it is a good idea to have only tea or coffee and soft drinks on the reception buffet. Then, when the bride is ready to cut the cake, glasses of champagne can be carried round. Very few bottles will be drunk under these circumstances.

LONG SPEECHES AT A WEDDING

Food

It is quite unnecessary at an afternoon reception to have anything more substantial than sandwiches and small attractive pastries. Ices have become popular in the last few years.

Changing to go away

The bride goes upstairs to change as soon as she has finished cutting the cake. Only her mother or sisters go with her. Traditionally she throws her bouquet from the top of the stairs to the bridesmaids and the one who catches it will be the next bride.

When the bride comes down in her travelling clothes, she and the bridegroom—who has also changed—leave immediately. The bride kisses her parents and parents-in-law, then runs to the car while being showered with rice and rose petals.

Rice is symbolic of fertility, rose petals of happiness. Confetti is messy and common and should not be thrown.

The evening after the wedding

Sometimes the bridesmaids are asked out by the best man and the ushers to dinner after the wedding. Unless the bridegroom is very rich, the men each pay their share for the evening.

Announcement in the press

The day after the wedding it is usual for an announcement to appear on the front page of *The Times*. This will cost 24s. for three lines and 8s. for each additional line.

The announcement should be made as follows:

SMITH-WHITLOCK. On May 9th. 1961, at the Parish Church, Essendon, Hatfield by the Canon H. Lovell, David Lawrence, youngest son of Major and Mrs Smith of 115, Hyde Park Street, W.2. and Ethel,

... SHOWERED WITH RICE AND ROSE PETALS

only daughter of Mr and Mrs Whitlock of Rose Cottage, Essendon.

Society weddings are published in the Court Circular. These cost a lot of money and arrangements must be made with the Social Editress of *The Times* for them to be included.

Royal guests

If Royalty attend the wedding, or are represented, they are met at the church door before the bride arrives by the clergyman officiating and escorted to the front seat, while the congregation stand.

When the bride and bridegroom come down the aisle, they stop just before they reach the front pew and the bride curtsies, the bridegroom bows. They are followed by the bridesmaids who all curtsy.

The Royal personage is then escorted down the aisle by the officiating clergyman before anyone else leaves the pews.

Marrying again

A widow, or a woman who marries again does not wear a white wedding dress. But a girl who marries a widower may do so. A bouquet can always be carried at a second wedding but it should not be of white flowers. If the wedding is at a Registry Office it is usual for the bride to wear a spray of orchids or other coloured flowers instead of carrying a bouquet.

If there is a church service a widow is given away by her father, her brother or, sometimes, her son. She does not have bridesmaids or pages.

Wedding anniversaries

The first anniversary to be celebrated is the Silver Wedding. Silver being out of fashion, friends mostly send flowers and telegrams while the family of the happy couple give more useful gifts.

So many people ask what the anniversaries are; here is a list:

PAPER WEDDING—first year
WOODEN WEDDING—fifth year
TIN WEDDING—tenth year
LEATHER WEDDING—twelfth year
CRYSTAL WEDDING—fifteenth year
CHINA WEDDING—twentieth year
SILVER WEDDING—twenty-fifth year
IVORY WEDDING—thirtieth year
WOOLLEN WEDDING—fortieth year
SILK WEDDING—forty-fifth year
GOLDEN WEDDING—fiftieth year
DIAMOND WEDDING—sixtieth year

It is not usual to make any press announcement except for Golden and Diamond Wedding anniversaries—and even then it might be considered ostentatious unless relatives arrange for the insertion in a local newspaper. The normal procedure is to give details as under:

50TH WEDDING ANNIVERSARY
SMITH: On June 1, 1912, at St Mary's, Hightown, William Smith to Betty Jones. Present address: The Manor, Low Road, Downtown, Dorset.

In no circumstances should a motto, proverb or verse appear. Efforts of local newspapers to increase their revenue by persuading the relatives of long-married couples to insert congratulations are to be deprecated.

As regards celebrations, these should be wholly family affairs, with the possible exceptions of an invitation to a handful of very old friends.

Eleven

BIRTHS AND CHRISTENINGS

Announcements

A birth of a child is usually announced in *The Times* and *The Daily Telegraph*. It is very important that the wording should be traditional:

> CLARKE   On May 11th. 1961, at Queen Charlotte's Hospital, to Joan, wife of James Clarke—a son.

It is absolutely incorrect to put 'née Brown' after the mother's name, to say 'the gift of a son' or to put 'a sister for John.'

Many couples who adopt a child now have a formal announcement inserted under the BIRTHS column and most newspapers accept this form of announcement. It is an excellent way of informing friends that a child has been adopted and is done, of course, when the formalities are completed.

A typical announcement would be:

> JONES (adoption)   By Joan and David Jones, The Manor, High Road, Hightown, a son (David John), now eight months old.

It will be noted that as this is a legal entry into motherhood the wife's name is put first.

Less happy—and fortunately very rare these days—is the need to inform friends that a tragedy occurred at birth. Because embarrassment and sorrow are minimised by giving the information as quickly and widely as possible, many couples do announce the fact. Such an announcement would read:

BROWN On June lst. 1961, at The Limes Maternity Home, Bournemouth, to Mary, wife of John Brown, a son (stillborn).

BIRTHS AND CHRISTENINGS

Birth announcement cards

Visiting cards with a tiny one tied in the corner with the child's name on it are never sent by anyone interested in etiquette. Nor are pictures of storks.

There is no need to notify anyone except the grandparents, who are telephoned by the husband from the hospital, and very intimate friends. Flowers sent to the hospital must all be thanked for by the wife as soon as she is well enough.

Registration of births and christenings

The birth of a child must, of course, be registered at the local offices within six weeks of the birth (in Scotland three weeks). Usually the birth is registered within a day or so. The birth certificate must be kept carefully, as the child will need to refer to it constantly during his life.

Christenings

Roman Catholics normally have to see that their children are baptised not later than the eighth day after birth when the urgent nature of the ceremony and the convalescence of the mother will mean that it is virtually a private affair.

In the Church of England most babies are between three and six weeks old when they are baptised. The father should approach the local incumbent to arrange the date and time for the christening, which is usually on a Sunday afternoon.

Godparents

The selection of godparents is an entirely personal matter between the parties concerned. But embarrassment may be caused by the proud father asking someone of importance who really does not know the family personally to act as a godparent, unless he has expressed a willingness beforehand.

By custom a boy has two godfathers and one godmother and a girl, two godmothers and one godfather. However most children in these days have two godmothers and godfathers.

Proxy godparents

The church has no objection to a proxy acting on behalf of a godparent who cannot be present. The proxy must be of the same sex as the absent godparent.

Godparents' duties

There are no religious or social objections to either married or single persons acting as godparents though for obvious reasons it is unusual to invite elderly people to take on this duty.

Despite the unfortunate trend towards regarding godparentage as a purely social matter, it should never be forgotten that the sole point of it is to guide and control the child's spiritual life. These responsibilities continue until the child is confirmed. Godparents are also expected to send their godchildren a gift at Christmas.

Guests

Invitations to a christening are normally kept to an absolute minimum and for this reason it is quite unnecessary to have printed cards, though if relatives are numerous and the birth of a child is of some local importance — i.e. perhaps the son of a Member of Parliament— then 'At Home' cards can be used.

After the christening

It is usual for the guests at a christening ceremony to be invited to the home of the parents afterwards. As in the overwhelming number of cases the christening is in the afternoon, the invitation should include wording to the effect that tea will be provided. For most christenings a personal and brief letter from the mother will be sufficient. Replies to the invitation should be sent immediately on receipt.

Precedence at christenings

At the church the guests take pews near the font unless they are very close relatives such as grandparents of the baby or, of course, the godparents. The most important godmother is responsible for holding the child and takes up her position on the left of the priest.

All godparents stand close to the child and in due course answer the question as to whether they renounce 'the Devil and all his works' on behalf of the baby.

The godmother who holds the baby tells the clergyman the name, and after the child has been baptised it is handed back to her. The father goes into the vestry, sees that the child is registered and makes a small gift of money to the church funds.

Back at home a simple tea is provided, usually of the stand-up variety, the only special item being a Christening Cake. The guests should not stay more than an hour.

Christening gifts

No one except the godparents is expected to give a baby a present, but it is usual to take a woolly coat or a soft toy. The godparents can offer a traditional present—a silver knife, fork and spoon, a silver mug engraved with the child's name or some simple piece of jewellery which the child can treasure all its

life. In these days, however, wealthy godparents often give money to be deposited in
a savings bank. This fund can in later years be
increased by birthday and Christmas gifts.

The cake

It is nice if it is possible for the decorations of
the christening cake to have some special
significance. For my eldest son's christening
cake I chose a Scottish castle with my husband's
Skian-dhu stuck in the top.

If close relatives or friends, and particularly
a godparent, regret their inability to attend the
christening, it is a nice thought to send them
small pieces of the cake in the same way that
pieces of wedding cake are sometimes des-
patched.

Choice of names

It is perhaps a waste of time to make any
suggestions about the appropriate names for
children, as parents tend to be very obstinate
in their choice, but as a postscript to the
etiquette of Christenings it might not be
inappropriate to point out the social and
psychological importance of selecting names
with care.

The majority of people are given two names
while three will cause little comment. Four,
however, unless there are very good family
reasons for them, should be avoided.

It need hardly be pointed out that names of ephemeral interest at the time of the baby's birth will be greatly resented in later years. Many an unfortunate adult has gone through life enduring the name of some politician, actress, newly crowned monarch or other famous personality who happened to be in the public eye at the time of his birth.

Parents should also reject names which can be easily shortened into something ugly or comical. And the unusual and bizarre names should also be avoided.

There is a lot to be said for the Roman Catholic idea of using names from a list approved by the Church and the refusal of the priests to christen children with any other.

Twelve

BEREAVEMENTS

Correct behaviour at the time of death in the family, and by friends and relatives of the deceased, is not merely a social obligation but a method of softening the grief with sympathy and kindness.

Sorrow is inevitable and cannot be eradicated by pretending to ignore the death or of getting the funeral over with the minimum of fuss and trouble.

Telegrams

First one has to inform those who will want to know about the death. For relatives at a distance who cannot be reached by telephone a short telegram should say: 'Deeply regret Aunt Doris died 10 o'clock this morning.'

Letters

For other relatives and friends a letter may be sent including, if it is wished that the recipient should attend the funeral, some details of when it will take place.

Press announcements

The announcement of the death should be, if possible, in the press the following day. This gives friends of the deceased time to make arrangements to get to the funeral. An insertion in the front page of *The Times* under Deaths, costs 24s. for three lines and 8s. for each additional line. The correct wording is:

BURY—On May 10th. 1961 at The Towers, Broadway, Worcestershire, ARTHUR FREDERICK BURY, O.B.E., aged 72, beloved husband of Marjorie. Funeral at St Mary's Church, Broadway, on Friday, May 15th., at 11.30 a.m.

Alternatively, you can put:

'service at the Broadway Parish Church tomorrow (Thursday) at 5 p.m. followed by cremation (private)'

No flowers by request

Some people want no flowers to be sent, in which case you add: 'No flowers by request'.

Others add special requests, such as: 'No flowers, but donations may be sent to Cancer Research Fund.'

Letters of condolence

These are written to the widow or widower and should not contain anything which does not concern the person who is dead. Here, for example, is a formal letter to the wife of a local Councillor:

278

Dear Mrs Smith,

My husband and I send you our deepest sympathy and condolence in your sad loss. Your husband will be sadly missed by his colleagues, but I know that the magnificent work he has done for the town will be long remembered, while his splendid example will be an inspiration to those who follow him.

Our thoughts are with you and your family at this tragic time.

Yours sincerely,

Wreaths

Flowers in the form of a wreath or a sheaf should be sent for the funeral. No one carries them personally; they are delivered by the local florist or from the station. Today it is not absolutely essential that the flowers should be white.

A visiting card is attached to the wreath. The woman's is used on which is engraved 'Mrs Alan Black'. In her own writing she adds 'Mr and'. Above the names the words 'With deepest sympathy' are written. If the deceased is a close friend, the mourner crosses out the formal names with a single line and writes 'With love and in affectionate memory from Alan and Joan'.

If you have no visiting card, then use a plain

florist's card—not one edged with black—and write on it: 'With the deepest sympathy of Mr and Mrs Alan Black' or 'With love and affectionate memory from Alan and Joan Black'.

Over-demonstrative messages are not correct.

Attendance at funerals

Those attending funerals should respect the request of 'no mourning' if that has been made, but they will of course wear sombre clothes. Where there is no ruling, mourning is obviously expected.

At most funerals men still wear morning coats with black waistcoats, black ties and black top hats, or when the funeral is in winter, they often wear a dark suit, their overcoat and a top hat. A black or grey suit, a black tie and black shoes can be worn at a quiet funeral.

Mourning arm bands

These are worn only by the armed services when ordered to do so; by organised bands of people such as football teams, but never by individuals.

The ceremony

The custom of today as regards the funeral ceremony itself is to make it as simple as possible. There will normally be two services,

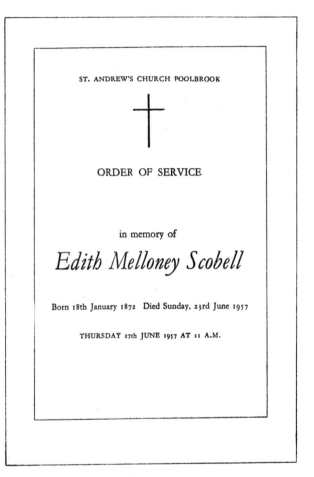

ST. ANDREW'S CHURCH POOLBROOK

ORDER OF SERVICE

in memory of

Edith Melloney Scobell

Born 18th January 1872   Died Sunday, 23rd June 1957

THURSDAY 27th JUNE 1957 AT 11 A.M.

FORM OF SERVICE AT A FUNERAL

one at the parish church and one at the grave-side.

The service in the church is printed on a folder of four sheets. It is quite correct for the outside to have a narrow black or purple line round the lettering and a small cross underneath the name of the church.

Precedence in the church

The order of precedence at the church service gives way to the relationship with the deceased. Members of the family drive off in the first car.

If the body is to be interred in a cemetery away from the church or is to be cremated, only the family mourners follow.

The rest of the congregation should stay in their places in the church until the funeral procession has moved outside and the vehicles have drawn away.

Memorial services

Memorial services take place a week or more after the funeral. If Royalty is represented the officiating clergyman meets the representatives at the door and escorts them to the front pew while the congregation stands. After the service the representative leaves first, escorted by the clergyman to his car.

The only intimation people receive of a Memorial Service—except of course the intimate relatives—is a notice in the newspapers. This should read as follows:

> BARRINGTON — A Memorial Service for the Hon. John Edward Barrington will be held at St. James's Church, Abbey Road, S.W.7. on Wednesday, May 30th. at 11 a.m.

Answering letters of condolence

After the funeral and within three weeks of the death letters of sympathy should be answered by the widow or the children of the deceased.

Printed cards

It is quite wrong to send printed cards of thanks for letters of condolence and flowers. This should never be done. If the person who has died is very important and there are literally thousands of letters, the following notice can be put at the top of the Personal Column of *The Times*:

> 'Lady X wishes to thank all those who have written to her on the death of her husband. She will reply to each one personally as soon as possible.'

Another version is:

> 'Mrs A. B. was deeply touched by the kind letters and lovely flowers sent to her on her

recent bereavement. She will reply personally as soon as possible.'

Period of mourning

Outward signs of grief shown by prolonged periods of mourning are not now so conventional as they were. Six months for a husband and three months for a child are the usual times of deep mourning; while for aunts, uncles or cousins, mourning is usually discarded after a month or, in many cases, after the funeral.

In memoriam

Many people wish to remember their relations on the anniversary of their death by putting a notice in the 'In Memoriam' column of *The Times* or *The Daily Telegraph*. As in notices of death it is incorrect to add frills or sentimental messages. Here is notice which is inserted every year by my mother:

CARTLAND — In loving memory of my husband MAJOR BERTRAM CARTLAND, killed at Berry-au-Bac, May 27th. 1918; and of my eldest son MAJOR RONALD CARTLAND, M.P., killed at Cassel, May 30th. 1940; also of my younger son CAPTAIN ANTHONY CARTLAND, killed near Ypres, May 29th. 1940.

Thirteen

ETIQUETTE ON PUBLIC OCCASIONS

Nowadays, sooner or later, everyone has to undertake duties which are, in effect, public work. It may be just to second a motion at a ratepayers' meeting or it may be some small but significant part in a ceremony with Royalty or distinguished guests present.

'Royalty! When will I ever meet Royalty?' a woman asked me scornfully when I told her I was writing this chapter.

Three weeks later she rang me up and said:

'You must be clairvoyant! You won't believe it but Princess Margaret is coming to visit the Health Clinic where I work part-time, and I'm to be presented to her!'

Committee work

Introduction to public work will more often than not be on a committee. Get over that stile and the rest will not be so difficult, for time and experience will indicate how things are done.

On important committees, taking the word in its widest sense, things are not too difficult for a newcomer. The new J. P. has the Clerk of the Court to guide and advise him. In that most intricate and tradition-controlled committee of all — the House of Commons — the Whips and many of the servants of the House will see that all goes well for the newly-elected Member.

But on the committee of the local Golf Club, the Women's Institute, the various branches of Church activity, there will be no full-time paid secretary or clerk to provide unpaid service. And yet the newcomer will soon find that customs and unwritten rules are rigidly observed.

Types of committee

Committees which interest ordinary people are of two kinds. The first is formed to attain an objective and will end when that objective is attained. It could be to send a local residents' protest about a new by-pass, to organise an old folks' outing or run a Sunday School sports day. The members of such a committee are responsible to themselves and themselves only.

The second, and more usual, is the executive body of a group — of a charity, sports club, the Women's Institute, Townswomen's Guild, Local Residents' Association. This committee in theory never ceases to exist and only its membership changes.

The chairman

In the case of many groups the President is automatically the Chairman of the committee. If not, a Chairman has to be elected by the committee members and not by the general members. It is usual also to appoint an honorary secretary and, if money is involved, an honorary treasurer. Other officers depend, of course, on the nature of the duties involved.

A good Chairman, it has been said, is one who just sits in the chair. Undoubtedly, a Chairman should talk little and confine himself

A TYPICAL COMMITTEE

principally to curbing the prosy and argument-
ative speeches of others. Nothing is more
annoying for a visiting Speaker, like myself,
than a Chairman who makes my speech for
me!

I often long to imitate the first Earl of
Birkenhead. He was at a meeting where the
Chairman, having talked for over an hour,
finished with:

'Lord Birkenhead will now give you his
address.'

Lord Birkenhead rose and said:

'My address is 32, Grosvenor Gardens,
West 1', and sat down.

A Chairman should welcome the Speaker,
introduce him or her by giving — briefly — a
description of their work and achievements
and the reason they are present, and then he
should sit down.

To make a Chairman's job easier I always
send a postcard to the Secretary of the organisation giving a few short details about myself.
I started this after a visit to Cambridge where,
just before I rose to present a number of cups
to the St John's Ambulance Brigade Cadets, the
Chairman said rather glumly that he knew
nothing about me.

I told him a few details quickly and then he
rose and said:

'Miss Barbara Cartland tells me that she has
written 80 books. I hope she will stop there!'

If your Speakers or important guests do not send you any information about themselves it is wise to write and ask them for details which will be helpful. *Who's Who* is also a great help.

At the end of the Speaker's address the Chairman says: 'I will now call on Mrs Jones to propose a vote of thanks for the delightful speech which we have all enjoyed.'

The secretary

The honorary secretary has invaluable work to do. Accuracy, precision and a veneration of correct routine are the qualities he needs.

The Chair rules almost dictatorially over the meeting, controls and selects speakers, gives verdicts on points of order (which must not be disputed), provides information, and summarises members' views.

The secretary prepares the minutes, agenda and other arrangements, keeps members informed, deals with correspondence and carries out actions decided on by the committee.

When visiting speakers come to the local Women's Institutes or to any other organisation, the secretary should make sure that the visitor has a train time-table and is met at the station or is given a route by which to find the hall. If he has come by car, a parking place must also be kept for him.

Agenda

The agenda for a meeting must be sent to all members well in advance of the date. A typical example would be:

NEWTOWN GOLF CLUB

A meeting of the committee will be held in the Club House on January 1st. 1962 at 3 p.m. at which your kind attendance is requested.

Business.

1. Minutes of the last meeting.
2. Business arising from minutes.
3. Groundsman's report.
4. Appointment of new committee members.
5. Proposed Easter competition.
6. Any other business.

The Chairman's task is to see that committee members adhere to the agenda. Under 'any other business' someone is liable to bring up matters of considerable importance. The Chairman may, in that case, ask the member to defer it until the next meeting when it can be put on the agenda.

The minutes

A secretary must keep the minutes. Any resolution passed, or course of action agreed upon, should be read aloud to obtain the approval of all concerned. The names of the proposer and seconder and how the resolution was passed or rejected, must be included. Those who contribute details of importance should be noted.

Minutes are written up as soon as possible after the meeting and shown to the Chairman for approval.

Members who attend should sign their names in an attendance book, and these names are included in the minutes for reading at the next meeting. Apologies received for absence are also included.

The quorum

Committees should decide at the outset the number which will constitute a quorum; below which the meeting will be cancelled. (The word originates from the word 'four' and this, it may be assumed, is the absolute minimum).

The meeting

The Chairman and the secretary should be at the meeting place ahead of the scheduled time. Members should be early rather than late, and the Chairman is entitled to open the proceedings at the scheduled hour so long as the quorum is present, and notwithstanding the absence of an important member.

Voting

Voting at committee meetings is carried out by the Chairman asking: 'Will anyone put a motion?' (a useful way of curbing a dilatory discussion) or by a member asking if he may do so. Someone will second it, and then the vote is put to the meeting, voting being usually by a show of hands.

A Chairman can put a motion himself, and a seconder is then not needed, in cases where no argument or dissent is probable. For instance, in cases of votes of sympathy for a sick member or condolence to the relatives of a deceased one.

In most committees the Chairman has the casting vote. The secretary, provided he is unpaid, may vote; but the treasurer is invariably an *ex officio* member and cannot vote.

Sub-committees

Sub-committees are regularly formed. They offer a simple solution for a small organisation with much to do—as, for instance, if a golf club is organising a big tournament.

By appointing Publicity, Entertainment Handicapping and Ladies sub-committees much interminable work will be avoided by the main committee.

The chair

At formal meetings every member, except the

Chairman, must rise before speaking. **All**
remarks are addressed to the Chair, and other
members are referred to in the third person.
The Chairman must be addressed as Mr
Chairman — or Madam Chairman — and not
by name.

Speeches

The great art of making a successful speech is
to be brief. It is difficult to generalise but this
is a guide:

Opening a Bazaar or Fête when the audience
is standing, 3 to 5 minutes.

Opening a Bazaar or Fête when the audience
is sitting, 5 to 7 minutes.

Proposing or replying to a toast at a dinner
or luncheon, 10 minutes maximum.

Giving away prizes at a School, Horticultural Show etc., 5 minutes maximum.

A perfect sermon, 10 minutes.

Preparing a speech

The first thing to remember is that a speech
should be absolutely sincere. Never speak on
anything that doesn't interest you — never
speak just to be funny.

You must have a good beginning and a good
ending. Light and shade is also important—
so you want to insert a little gaiety, an amusing
story, followed by warm-hearted sincerity
about the cause or reason for which you are

speaking. The main rule is to stick to the subject.

One thing in which I firmly believe is that you should never make a speech without giving the audience 'something to take away'. I don't mean that you should sermonise but try to include in every speech something worthwhile.

For newcomers

Prepare your speech with care, think it out, write it out, time it and then learn it by heart.

GIVING AWAY PRIZES AT A HORTICULTURAL SHOW

When you think you have it word perfect, put down the heading of each paragraph on a postcard. Take this with you on the platform or to the table and, in case you think you may forget, glance at it occasionally.

Don't say this is too much trouble. Sir Winston Churchill always writes out his speeches, even including pauses for laughter or cheers.

Appearance

When you are speaking remember not to fidget. Nothing is more annoying than to watch a speaker taking his glasses on and off, fiddling with his tie or putting his hands in and out of his pockets. It distracts from what he is saying.

Stand absolutely still. Do not sway from foot to foot. Keep your hands either clasped together or rest them on the table. A man can put one hand in his coat pocket. Speak directly to the far end of the room, making certain in this manner that you throw your voice to the person farthest away. Practise all this in front of a looking-glass.

Voice

Do speak slowly and clearly. If you know anyone with a tape-recorder, borrow it and hear your own voice. It will give you a shock!

A Dinner and Dance

A Dinner and Dance has become a popular mode of entertainment. The guests pay for their dinner and important speakers usually charge nothing or just their expenses. Guests pay for their own drink and that of their guests. The top table has drink provided either by the Chairman or out of their funds.

The menu is usually a four-page folder and has the name and crest of the Association, Charity or Organisation on the outside, with the date, the place and the name of the Chairman. Inside, the Menu is on page 1, opposite the Toasts:

TOASTS

H.M. THE QUEEN

Proposed by	The President

THE LOCAL EDUCATION AUTHORITY

Proposed by	A.E.R. Otter Esq.
Response by	County Councillor John Chear

THE NATIONAL UNION OF TEACHERS

Proposed by	The Rt Hon. J. Chuter-Ede, C.H., J.P., D.L., M.P.
Response by	Cedric Griggs Esq.

296

OUR GUESTS

Proposed by	The President
Response by	County Councillor
	Mrs Hugh
	McCorquodale

Addressing the audience

There is often some confusion as to the opening of a speech. The Chairman always comes first. The Speaker therefore says, in this order: 'Mr. Chairman, Your Royal Highness, Your Grace, Your Excellencies, My Lords, Ladies and Gentlemen...' or: 'Madam Chairman, Madam President, Ladies...'

Seating of the guest of honour

At all public occasions, the guest of honour, even when he or she is Royal, sits on the right of the Chairman. On all municipal occasions, whether for business or entertainment, the Mayor should preside or act as host.

Lord Lieutenants and High Sheriffs

Lord Lieutenants and High Sheriffs have first place in their own County during their tenure of office, the Lord Lieutenant taking precedence over the High Sheriff; and both have precedence within their jurisdiction over a Mayor, even within his own Borough, when both are present officially on a County occa-

sion. Once they cross the border into another
County they lose all precedence.

Reference to the Queen

In a speech one refers to the Queen as 'Her
Majesty' or 'The Queen'—never as 'she'. In
talking to the Queen one says, 'Ma'am'—as to
all other Royal ladies. One does not say 'your
wife' to the Duke of Edinburgh, or 'your
sister' to Princess Margaret.

Reference to males of the Royal Family

Where the male members of the Royal Family
are concerned, one says 'Your Royal Highness'
or 'the Duke' and 'Sir' in conversation.

A Royal visit

If you are honoured by the visit of a member
of the Royal Family to your town, your hospital, Fête or anything in which you are Chairman, the following is the procedure. Let us
pretend that the Queen Mother attends a country Fête you have arranged in aid of some
National Charity. All arrangements will have
been made with Her Majesty's Controller.
When you invited the Queen Mother in the
first place, you will have written to him at Cla-
rence House asking if it would be possible for
Her Majesty to honour your project.

The Controller will inform you that Her

Majesty will be graciously pleased to visit you and he will specify the time she will arrive.

A list of guests whom you would like to present to Her Majesty must be submitted to the Controller, also if Her Majesty is having luncheon or tea during the visit, the guests you would wish invited to that meal.

County police, of course, must be informed and permission must be asked of the Controller before any announcement of Her Majesty's visit can be sent to the press.

If the Queen Mother is expected to arrive at 3 o'clock, she will be there exactly on time. You, as Chairman, will meet her on the steps of a private house or the Town Hall with the Mayor, the Lord Lieutenant of the County, the High Sheriff and the President of the organisation you are sponsoring. If you are a woman, your curtsy to the Queen Mother is *as low as possible*. You keep your back straight, your head up and look her straight in the face. It is not correct to bow the head.

Do practise this before the great day. When I attend a film première I am horrified to see how badly and how clumsily the film stars and the majority of those presented curtsy to Her Majesty. Most of them just bob, stretching out their behinds and bowing their heads.

A man stands almost to attention and bows his head from the neck only. To bow from the waist is incorrect.

You address the Queen Mother as 'Ma'am'. You then escort Her Majesty through the house or building to the Fête itself. Here, as soon as she appears, the band plays 'God Save The Queen' and all stand to attention. You can then have a long list of presentations, taking good care not to forget the secretaries, who will have worked very hard for the cause, even if they have been paid.

Be careful to say the name of each person clearly and, if possible, to describe what they have done to help.

When the presentations are over, the Queen Mother will go round some of the stalls or exhibits; but this should all have been arranged beforehand and the police will keep clear the way ahead of her.

When the tour is over, the Queen Mother should be given tea with important dignitaries of the County, the organisation and the Charity, in the house, Town Hall or a special marquee.

Then when Her Majesty is ready to leave, you, with the other members of the reception committee, escort her to her car, line up to say good-bye, curtsy as she shakes hands and again as the car drives away.

Even if you are not so fortunate as to have Royalty at anything you organise, the principle of looking after your guest of honour is almost exactly the same.

Always remember that the visiting celebrity wants to meet as many people as possible and that everyone wants to meet him or her.

Chairmen of committees are often very selfish and keep the star to themselves. I have seen the late Countess Mountbatten, who was wonderful on these occasions, break away from the officials around her to talk to a cleaner in a hospital or some ordinary spectator who never dreamt of being noticed.

The important thing on such occasions is the 'personal touch' and I am sure that most people would rather meet the celebrity than just listen from a distance.

Collecting the purchases

The Chairman should not leave the distinguished guest from the time he or she arrives until the time they leave. If you are in charge of a Bazaar, it is wise to arrange that a man or boy follows the Opener round the stalls to carry the things she buys.

When I open a Bazaar or Fête, I buy something at every stall. It is impossible for me to carry the purchases myself and I feel embarrassed if my Chairman or the Mayor, who may be with me, becomes laden with pots of jam and trays of eggs.

Introductions

Do not forget to introduce the Opener to the

Treasurer, who is usually working in a room apart, and the ladies who are serving the tea and washing up.

Total amount raised

When the amount raised is known, it is the Chairman's or the Secretary's job to write to the Opener telling her 'the good news', and at the same time enclosing any reference there may have been to the function in the local newspapers.

Bouquets

At a Bazaar, Fête or Sale of Work, the Opener is traditionally given a bouquet, usually presented by a reluctant child whose mother hisses 'curtsy' unavailingly. If the Opener has to return home by train, or is staying the night locally, a bouquet is obviously an inconvenience. The organiser should then see that, instead, a box of chocolates or a small gift characteristic of the town is presented.

Bouquets, for some unknown reason, are never given at a dinner or a luncheon, which are usually far more hard work for the Guest of Honour if she has to make a speech. I think, if the speaker does not ask for a fee, a gift of some sort is only good manners on the part of the organisation which has issued the invitation.

Vote of thanks

At a Bazaar or Meeting, the person who makes
an ordinary vote of thanks should thank the
Speaker and nothing else. Sometimes they are
far too inclined to make a speech about themselves or tell stories. They should not take more
than two minutes and refer only to those they
have to thank. This is, of course, distinct from

... A BOUQUET ...

the 'Vote of Thanks' made at a dinner or luncheon when this is merely an excuse to have another speaker on the Toast List.

Coffee morning

Coffee mornings have become so popular in the last year that I must explain the etiquette of these.

Being lent a house. It is usual to ask the owner of one of the largest houses in the village, or someone with a fair-sized house in town if they will have a coffee morning in their house. If they agree, the organiser offers to provide the coffee and the milk and sugar. This, however, is usually given by the same person who lends the house.

A leaflet. Friends of the organiser and those helping her are notified either by letter or leaflet that the coffee morning is taking place. If it is by leaflet, it is worded something like this:

In Aid of the Centenary Appeal for
The Queen's Institute of District Nurses.
A Coffee Morning
will be held
on

Tuesday, June 14th., at 11 a.m.
at
The Cedars, Hertfordbury
(by kind permission of Mrs H. Lang)
Please bring something and buy something.

Making of cakes. The organiser and the ladies who are helping her then make the cakes, biscuits and scones which are sold with the cups of coffee, 1/- being the usual inclusive charge.

Speech of thanks. When a number of people are present, it is usual for the organiser to say a few informal words, explaining the worthiness of the cause they are supporting. In her speech she must thank Mrs Lang for lending the house and the ladies who made all the arrangements and those who have contributed the cakes, biscuits etc.

Washing up. The organiser and her ladies must also offer to help make and serve the coffee and wash up the cups and plates afterwards. If Mrs Lang has a staff of her own and they do the washing up, then a small tip should be provided out of the funds.

Women's clothes

I get many letters from the wives of Mayors, Chairmen of Councils and other civic posts asking me what clothes they should wear during their husband's term of office. They must, of course, look attractive but there is no need to be extravagant.

Dresses

They will want a smart evening dress for evening receptions. This should be long, and if as Lady Mayoress they wear a gold chain, it should not be over-decorated with beads or sequins. Certain colours such as blue, green and white go particularly well with gold jewellery. For the daytime they will require an afternoon dress, a cocktail dress and several hats.

Hats

I cannot stress too often that on every formal occasion, whether it is a Luncheon, a Bazaar or a Meeting, a hat should be worn. At any time I hate middle-aged women, with greying hair blowing untidily in the breeze; but it is worse when they are in the focus of public interest. The women Chairman, Secretary and Treasurer of any Meeting—and anyone else who is on the platform—should always wear hats.

Gloves

When receiving at an evening reception, the President or Chairman's wife should wear long gloves. Any colour is permissible. It is now correct, since the Queen does it, to wear a bracelet outside the gloves, but not a ring.

Decorations

Insignia, Decorations and Medals may be worn with morning dress on official occasions and at public functions. Miniatures are worn in the evening and it is usual to wear them only on a tail coat—but King George VI approved as a temporary measure Miniatures being worn with dinner jackets by those not in possession of full evening dress.

The following are the occasions upon which Orders, Miniatures, Decorations and Medals are to be worn with full evening dress:

1. At all official parties and dinners when any of the following Members of the Royal Family are present:

> The Queen
> Queen Elizabeth, the Queen Mother
> The Duke of Edinburgh
> The Princess Margaret, and the Earl of Snowdon
> The Duke and Duchess of Gloucester
> The Princess Royal
> The Duke of Windsor
> Princess Marina, Duchess of Kent
> The Duke and Duchess of Kent
> The Princess Alexandra
> The Princess Alice, Countess of Athlone
> (For other members of the Royal Family ask the Controller what is correct before the ceremony).

2. At all parties and dinners given in houses of Ambassadors and Ministers, unless the guests are otherwise notified by the Ambassador or Minister concerned.
3. At all official Dinners and Receptions includ-

307

ing Naval, Military and Royal Air Force
Dinners, Dinners of City Livery Companies
and Public Dinners. (For all these the word
'Decorations' on the invitation card will
show if the entertainment is an official one).
4. On official occasions when entertained by:
  The Lord Lieutenant of a County within
  his County.
  The High Sheriff of a County within his
  County.
  Cabinet Ministers, Lord Mayors and
  Mayors.

Fourteen

OFFICE ETIQUETTE

Applying for a job

So many people apply for jobs in the wrong way. In the first place a letter should by typed or clearly written. It should give full particulars of your age, education, experience, previous posts, names and addresses of persons from whom a reference can be obtained, and arrangements when the applicant can be free for an interview.

The letter should end 'Yours respectfully' or 'Yours faithfully' according to the type of job required.

Looking one's best

When an interview is arranged it is most important to look one's best. I personally always look at a man's shoes. If he can't clean his own shoes, he is not likely to serve me very well. Men also forget that a smart head is a guide to character. Long hair looks slovenly or 'arty-crafty'. Too elaborate a style of hairdressing is suspicious.

Both men and women should watch their fingers. Dirty nails and nicotine-stained fingers are disgusting.

Being interviewed

A young man should be very punctilious in saying 'Sir' continually in addressing his future employer. He should stand until asked to sit down, and if his interviewer rises for some reason, he too must rise and remain standing until invited to sit down again.

Do not be over-voluble and tell long stories about yourself; but answer the questions intelligently and with just as much detail as is necessary.

Thanking the interviewer

On leaving, whether you have got the job or not, say thank-you for having been accorded an interview.

Also write a letter of thanks for being accorded an interview. A young man I know was interviewed for a very special job in a firm, which he hadn't got much hope of getting. As he expected he was turned down, but wrote a charming letter to the Managing Director thanking him for the interview.

A week later he was sent for by the same firm. 'Another position has fallen vacant through an accident,' he was told. 'We were so impressed at your good manners in writing to us that we thought you might be interested in filling this new vacancy.'

A woman's appearance

Women should always wear stockings at an interview and, if possible, a hat. It is a mistake to put on too much make-up and never add to it in the presence of someone you hope will be your future employer.

Jangling bracelets or drop ear-rings should not be worn, nor an inescapable scent.

Smells

Here I must warn a girl that scent is never a cover-up for any other smell. I had a lady's maid for a short time who knew I hated the smell of smoke. Therefore when she had been smoking she covered herself with a pungent scent. It was no disguise and the result was awful. Never use cheap scent at any time; much better buy a toilet water of an expensive make and use a little more. It works out about the same price and is infinitely more effective.

Addressing the interviewer

For all domestic purposes say 'Madam' to the lady interviewing you. Governesses and secretaries say 'Mrs X' but be careful not to sound familiar. It is always wiser to let one's future employer do the talking and not to volunteer information.

Letters of application

Here is a specimen letter from a girl applying for the post of a typist:

Telephone: From MISS ELLA BLOGGS,
Potters Bar 22432   24, Clacton Lane,
                           Potters Bar, Middx.

To The Manager,
The Easidoesit Co.,
24, Hoppet's Way,   1st. Jan. 1962
Finchley.

Dear Sir,

I wish to apply for the post of Secretary as advertised in the Barnet Press. I am 20 years old and have a shorthand speed of 120 words. I have worked for the 'Slow and Sure' Company in Potters Bar for two years, but they are moving into London. They will be pleased to give you a reference should you require one.

I was educated at Queen Elizabeth's Grammar School where I obtained my General Certificate of Education. If you will grant me an interview I shall be most grateful.

Yours faithfully,
Ella Bloggs.

Typed letters

I am continually astonished at would-be secretaries who, asking for a job, send me letters which are badly typed. They use a typing ribbon which is worn out, the letters have irregular lines and the sentences are wrongly punctuated. I also never interview people who write:

'Dear Madam, Kindly send me further particulars of the post you advertise in the Daily Telegraph. What wages, hours, holidays etc? Yours faithfully.'

This is definitely not the way to get a job which is worth having.

Work etiquette

Probably the most important years of an average girl's 'public life', and certainly all the years that matter of a man's life, are spent at work. To young people work etiquette is of paramount importance, for it can make or mar their careers. In later years, the secret of leadership can be found in correct behaviour to superiors, equals and juniors.

An industrial or commercial organisation in the final analysis is not unlike a unit of the armed services. Discipline, both in oneself and in others, makes for a 'happy ship' when fairly and justly imposed. Lack of discipline, masquerading as feckless friendship, makes for unhappiness.

A junior should avoid unsuitable dress even if the nature of the job suggests that what is worn can hardly matter. No matter how comfortable leisure clothes may be they are not symbols of efficient work.

Young men should eschew the extreme kinds of hair cut, bearing in mind that if promotion is desired appearance will count and it will be noted that none of the departmental heads or the managerial staff adopt such styles.

Bright ties, most of the Italian styles in tailoring and footwear, are unsuitable. So are gaudy pullovers, badges and jewellery. Most of all, cleanliness is essential. Young men in their teens often think that they can skip the daily shave. Probably they could at sixteen or seventeen; so they may believe that they can at a year or two later. Frankly if they have any self respect they can't. Particular attention should also be paid to clean nails.

Girl employees 'have never had it so good'. The result of the demand exceeding the supply of even semi-skilled clerical staff is that a terribly large number of teen-age typists behave like prima donnas or film stars—and dress like them.

Figure-accentuating dresses and jerseys, ultra-low cut styles, and footwear which makes walking both difficult and noisy, are among the allegedly attractive items of women's wear which have no place in an office.

Jewellery should be kept to a minimum. I know a man who got rid of a really efficient girl because the interminable jangling of her trinket-festooned bracelet as she typed sent him nearly insane.

Utter and meticulous cleanliness is vital. Most offices are small and kept very warm. The girl who offends the nostrils, either through body odour or the use of scents to disguise it, commits the cardinal sin—and will probably lose her job.

Good time-keeping is not a sign of slavish obedience but of respect for an employer's trust. Any employee would be extremely angry if the pay packet contained a few coppers less than it should, but lateness, and extra minutes on the lunch hour, and long visits to the cloakroom are merely methods of defrauding the employer out of the work it has been mutually agreed he shall pay for.

It is an old cliché that familiarity breeds contempt, but it is very true about work relationships. The office where everyone uses Christian names is frequently an inefficient office, even a discontented one.

Obviously girls on an equal footing will address one another by Christian names in direct conversation, but it is good manners to use the more formal address of 'Miss ...' when speaking to a girl on official matters in the presence of a superior.

Men may use Christian names through long association and on the grounds of equality; it is more masculine however for them to use the surname only. Superiors will use the surname only when addressing junior members of the staff, where the prefix of 'Mr' usually would suggest a formal and perhaps ominous conversation to come.

But older employees, say over twenty-five, will appreciate the courtesy of being addressed as 'Mr . . .' by superiors. This is again an example of smooth relationships taken from the army. A Field Marshal is always meticulously careful to address an N.C.O. he may know by name with his rank.

Executives who bawl surnames of the male employees or address a girl with the terse title of 'Miss' without the surname are demonstrating both their lack of manners and their feeling of not being up to their job without blustering about their own importance.

Juniors of both sexes addressing seniors cannot go wrong by using 'Sir'. In the United States this is almost universal and no one could charge the average American with being unduly deferential or emulating Uriah Heep.

Some executives may not like it, and will then courteously explain that they prefer to be addressed as 'Mr . . .'. Until that is explicitly stated no young employee can possibly go wrong by sticking to 'Sir' even if the other employees do not use the term.

Now that there are many women executives in business the problem of addressing them also arises. I believe that in some Civil Service departments a highly placed woman official has to be addressed as 'Ma'am' in the same way as officers in the women's services. I have not come across this practice in the commercial world, where the full title of 'Miss ...' or 'Mrs ...' is usual.

Some executives call their male staff and their girl secretaries by their Christian names, at least when visitors are not present. Personally I deprecate this, because it is somewhat difficult for a man who has shown that he prefers to be on terms of intimacy with someone to reprimand him or her when the need arises with the full impressiveness of his superior position.

In any event the employee should rigidly adhere to the formal address of 'Sir' or 'Mr ...'. I know of a rather puritanical German importer who came to discuss the financing of a British company which wanted to build a factory in Germany. This man abandoned negotiations simply because the British executive's secretary, asked to find some documents, tripped gaily into the conference room, laid the papers in front of her boss and said brightly; 'Here you are, Jim. They're all there.'

The German was completely convinced, albeit wrongly, that the girl was her employer's mistress, that the man was untrustworthy and probably in private financial difficulties!

317

References

If anyone changing a job wishes to give a previous employer's name as a reference, it is good manners to notify him or her, in a polite letter, hoping 'it will not be a trouble or inconvenience'. For References on Mortgages, Life Insurance etc., it is correct to ask permission before putting forward a name. The person who gives a reference must also be thanked afterwards.

Fifteen

MEMO ON MANNERS

Smoking

Smoking has become such a habit that people have the most extraordinary smoking manners without thinking what they are doing.

A man should never smoke without asking any lady present if he may do so, unless of course she herself is already doing so.

A man should not help himself to a cigarette without offering his case first to everyone else present.

A finished cigarette should not be thrown into the fire in somebody's sitting-room, nor the ash put in cups or on plates at meals. The late Marchioness of Londonderry once saw a debutante stub out a cigarette on the shaft of one of the marble statues at Londonderry House. She stopped the band, walked across the room and said:

'Would you be so kind as to use an ashtray to put out your cigarette?'

A finished cigarette should be stubbed out *completely* in an ashtray.

You should never enter a restaurant smoking a cigarette.

319

You should never enter a dining-room smoking a cigarette.

You should never enter a bedroom smoking a cigarette.

You should never smoke at dinner until after the port.

You should never smoke a pipe at a theatre

A DEBUTANTE STUBBING OUT HER CIGARETTE
ON A STATUE

or when a guest in a private house. Many women dislike pipe smoke and you should be quite certain your hostess is not one of these before asking if you may smoke.

At a dinner party you should wait to smoke until the host's cigarettes have been offered round. Cigarettes or cigars are smoked at dinners, never pipes.

Buttonholes

Englishmen are fond of buttonholes—which always surprises foreigners. A correct buttonhole is a red carnation unadorned by foliage or silver paper. Any other flower is affected or individualistic except at the Eton and Harrow match at Lords when all Harrovians wear cornflowers.

In a lift

Gentlemen always take their hats off in a lift if there is a lady passenger. They also stand back to let the lady leave first.

Telephone manners

I have a friend who keeps a shop. When I telephone, I am always in a temper long before I speak to her. Her staff are so disagreeable. It is absolutely essential for shops, businesses and private individuals to employ charming telephone operators and secretaries. Elizabeth Arden's shops say: 'Good morning!

This is Elizabeth Arden; can I help you?'

I choose my secretaries with soft, charming voices because they represent me.

'I'm so sorry, Miss Cartland out. I know she will be very sorry to miss you. If you will leave your number, I will ask her to telephone you as soon as she returns.' That is the sort of reply which pleases rather than:

'She's out!'

'When will she be back?'

'I don't know. You can try this evening.'

People with foreign servants are, however, helpless—all they can do is to teach them to say, like a parrot, into the telephone:

'Mrs out—back six,' and bang goes the receiver!

'MISSUS OUT ... BACK SIX'

Visiting cards

These are almost extinct except for business men; but if you do have one, it should be correct. For a woman a card is $3\,^1/_4$ inches in length and $2\,^1/_4$ inches in depth. The name is engraved in copper plate writing and the address is put in the left-hand corner.

A man's card should be 3 inches long and $1\,^1/_2$ inches deep. He has his address on the left and his Club on the right.

Decorations are never put on a business card.

If a married couple call on another married couple, the wife leaves one of her cards and her husband two. But as calling is out of date, private visiting cards are usually used only for wedding presents and wreaths.

Married couples in public

Nothing is worse manners than to sit in a restaurant with your husband or wife and say nothing. Married couples with dull, bored, sullen faces are all too familiar.

If you are out with your marriage partner, please make an effort to look amused and entertained. A French woman will always flirt with her husband in public, however long she has been married. To look bored is, after all, advertising the failure of your personal relationship, even if you remain tied together.

323

Clothes

Anthropologists have written that clothing was not originally worn for warmth but to symbolise status and to ensure modesty. An ancillary motive was sexual attraction—humanity discovering very early that concealment is more exciting than exposure.

Many women and quite a few men are in danger of forgetting or ignoring these basic

A FRENCHWOMAN WILL ALWAYS FLIRT WITH
HER HUSBAND IN PUBLIC

truths. Whatever your position wear the clothes appropriate to it; whatever the occasion see that clothes mark it. The clergyman in his dog collar, the Mayor in his robes, the engineer in his blue overalls, and the paratrooper in his zip-up denims all obey this law of clothes that are appropriate and indicative of the wearer's status.

In less strongly defined channels of living we can do the same. If it is an occasion for evening dress, wear it; if the event is informal, do not overdress. If you are over forty do not wear the styles of very young women. If you are young don't imagine that the attractiveness of youth will compensate for sloppy jeans and beatnik grime.

Cosmetics

Every woman with personal regard for herself makes use of cosmetics. Men, though they are slow to admit it, are gradually finding that it is socially necessary to make subtle use of cosmetics too—hair preparations, after-shave lotions and deodorants.

The first rule of using cosmetics is to make lavish use of the basic items—soap and water. The second rule is to make discreet use of all the rest.

Cosmetics are best used to try to attain a natural ideal, not to produce an unnatural effect. Thus lipstick is used to achieve the rosy redness which lips, in theory, should have naturally; it is not socially desirable to cause a sensation with mauve or dead white lips which in nature would insinuate an alarming state of health!

Similarly, bringing life to nails with some hue allied to their natural pink can cause no offence; colouring them green or black will cause offence—that it may be only to one's maiden aunt is not the point. Someone is offended and therefore the offender has shown bad manners.

Everyone knows that women use cosmetics, but that is no reason to advertise the fact or demonstrate the method of applying them in public. Repairs should always be a private matter, and not the inevitable finale to a restaurant meal or the preliminary before a move from indoors to outdoors and vice versa.

Going to the cloakroom

No man can understand why a girl he takes out to dinner—or his wife—spends so long in the cloakroom. I think it is the height of bad manners, yet time after time I take a party of debutantes to a dance and they spend half an hour in my bedroom before we leave the house, and after a twenty minute drive into the country, or five minutes in a taxi in London, they then stay in the cloakroom for another half an hour!

After a dinner party last year when I had twice sent upstairs to tell the girls we were ready to leave, I said, when they did appear:

'If you didn't look pretty before dinner, titivating for thirty minutes when we are all waiting isn't going to turn any of you into a Marilyn Monroe!'

My advice to a girl who wants to be a success is, slip out of the cloakroom quickly and the nicest young man in the party will undoubtedly ask you to dance.

REPAIRS SHOULD ALWAYS BE A PRIVATE MATTER

Sour faces

To me, a sour sulky face is extremely ill mannered. There is one rule for all people who want to be a success and that is, to smile.

'She may not be as pretty as she was,' a woman said of a spoilt society beauty, 'but at least she could look kind.'

Don't worry about your looks; worry instead if people fail to respond to your charm. Try to make them feel happy and at ease. Real good manners is not to be U or Non-U, not whether you say 'photo or photograph, not whether you cock your little finger over the tea-cup. It is if you make other people feel that the time they have spent with you has been well spent.

Say you don't know

If you don't know what to do, say so. It is only the very young and the pretentious who will never admit to being in a social predicament. Ask the person next to you what you should do, and he or she will be delighted. There is no-one in the world who can resist showing off superior knowledge.

For girls . . . look wide-eyed and appreciative and you will have got yourself a new admirer.

For young men . . . try asking the advice of an older man and you will have got yourself a patron.

Press photographs

Press photographers have become part of the
London scene and it is quite usual to allow them
to take photographs at balls and at private
dances. It is, however, extraordinarily bad
manners for a host and hostess to show off to
their friends by being rude in public to the
press.

The reporters often have a thankless job to
do and it is essential at all functions to which
they are invited, such as public and charity
luncheons, dinners, weddings and balls, that
they should be offered food and drink. Some
people have a 'Press Room' on these occasions
but personally I would not ask anyone to my
house who was not treated in exactly the same
way as everyone else.

At public functions, Civic luncheons and
dinners where guests pay for their wine, the
organising secretary must always see the press
is provided with drink. On many newspapers,
especially country ones, no expenses of this
sort are allowed and it is hard on a reporter to
have to pay for his drinks at a function he is
attending in the course of his duty—or make
himself conspicuous by drinking water.

It is not correct to have press photographs
taken of a house-party unless the important
guests — such as Cabinet Ministers, distinguished foreigners etc., — have been asked

beforehand and have given their permission. Nor is it considered 'the thing' by most sportsmen to have press photographs taken on the moors or at covert shoots.

Sports and pastimes

In Britain sport is almost a religion and pastimes can be formalised rituals. It is very easy for the newcomer to break the many unwritten laws which will offend even more than breaking the written regulations.

The taboos and conventions are so localised that it is quite impossible to enumerate them, and the best advice to anyone joining a golf club, going as a guest to a tennis club, or participating in a football or cricket match is to ask a close friend about local traditions and then to watch carefully how others behave.

Stephen Potter has written amusingly in his Gamesmanship and One-Upmanship books on the philistines of sport, and I recommend these books for hints on what not to do. It is also worth remembering that the British tradition in most games played for recreation is that the playing is the thing, and not the winning — a fact which exasperates foreigners but secretly intrigues them.

If invited to play tennis it is as fatuous to conceal the fact that one is a rabbit as to omit to mention that you were once considered for the Davis Cup.

If you are compelled to play, but are not very good, the fact that you genuinely try will be accepted as compensation for your sin in not being good at sport. If you are a potential champion conceal the fact as cleverly as you can. Don't be blatantly condescending, but, above all, don't blind your opponent with your skill and science.

... USELESS TO CONCEAL ONE IS A RABBIT

331

Men of any age are liable to be asked, almost commanded, to play cricket, football, golf, and any other game the host or neighbour likes, with the hearty rebuttal of excuses on the lines of 'it doesn't matter whether you can play; we just need someone else.'

Overbearing pressure on someone to play who obviously does not want to do so is bad manners, but to refuse so implicitly that an awkward silence ensues is even worse manners. It will be true enough that the quality of play will be ignored if poor, and only lightly praised if good.

The lore of sports costume would fill a book in itself. It best illustrates the English genius for careful nonchalance and for irrational and localised trends and traditions. These factors make it impossible to do more than generalise and the advice must once again be to study others.

For example, there are golf courses in Scotland where one can still see golfers wearing plus-fours and many wearing knickerbockers which went out of fashion farther south thirty and fifty years ago respectively. In the 'stockbrokers' belt' of the Home counties such wear would be both bizarre and curious, and there are strange laws at these clubs that a one-colour sweater of any hue is acceptable but a Fair Isle sweater isn't.

In some tennis clubs women wear very short

skirts, in others divided skirts, and in others skirts to the knees.

The growing enthusiasm for horse riding has far more rigid rules, even if they are unwritten. In some districts it would be regarded as ostentatious to wear the conventional riding habit; and slacks and sweaters for both sexes are *de rigueur*. In others the stables would probably find some excuse about no mounts being available if anyone turned up in anything but proper riding habit.

HORSE RIDING HAS RIGID RULES

Nowhere is it more essential than in sport to 'fit in'. This means wearing more or less exactly what the others do, so that the newcomer to a tennis or golf club, a riding stables or a cricket club, should make a discreet reconnaissance beforehand.

Ostentation either by overdressing on the one hand or sloppiness on the other should be avoided. The man who wears a yachting cap to sail his 14-ft dinghy round the bay may look ridiculous; without it at Cowes he would look equally absurd.

The girl who poses on the edge of a swimming pool in rather chilly Surrey in an abbreviated bikini is bad mannered, whereas in the South of France she would be in the fashion—providing, of course, that she has the sort of figure that makes a bikini attractive and not repulsive.

Remembering that in all sports the game's the thing and not the winning of it, one should observe that victory is not a reason for an exhibition of delight nor defeat a reason to sulk. Never query the verdict of umpire, referee or opponent no matter how blatantly wrong it appears to be. Being a good loser, even if the odds are unfair, is an example of good behaviour.

Personal gain should, generally speaking, never enter into sport—which means that it is usually bad manners to suggest a wager on the result. This certainly applies to all team games.

An exception to this general rule is that golfers who know one another well and have played together often enough to know their opponents' prowess may mutually agree on some kind of token bet. Even here the money involved should never be large enough to make winning worth while or losing a financial disaster.

Generally speaking, this restriction on the size of wagers applies to all indoor games. People who want to earn their living or jeopardise their income by playing bridge for money should join a club where they will meet people of the same outlook.

When bridge, whist, rummy and other card games are played in the home—usually as part of a social evening—stakes should be nominal, so that no one is likely to win or lose more than a shilling or two.

Beware of becoming a bridge or any kind of card game fiend or of inviting anyone of the species when entertaining people who may not have the same enthusiasm for cards. There is nothing more boring than spending the entire evening playing a game that does not particularly interest you and in opposition to an expert. The only worse situation is to have an expert as a partner.

Hosts who want to organise an evening of bridge should select guests with great care.

Guests whose idea of social bliss is to play rubber after rubber till 3 a.m. must try to remember that other people have other ideas of social activity.

If you do play cards, play them quietly. A running commentary interests no one and annoys everyone. Inquests on one's own good luck—or ill luck—and on one's partner's or opponents' play, are definitely to be deprecated. Cheating, which is surprisingly prevalent because the perpetrators fondly believe that they are undiscovered whereas it is the other people's good manners in keeping their thoughts to themselves, is definitely not done.

The magic formula

Last, but not least. If you have read this book carefully you will have discovered on almost every page the magic formula for good manners. It also ensures personal success and every possible advancement. It is to say 'thank you' and keep on saying it.

So... Thank you a thousand times for reading this.